How to Draw Backgr

BY MITCH LEEUWE

HI THERE !

Let me introduce myself. I'm Mitch Leeuwe and am an illustrator from the Netherlands. I always drew a lot as a kid. I even had the childhood dream to become an animator at Disney. During my teenage years, I lost that dream. Luckily, I slowly started drawing more and more. When I was 19, I began to do some freelance work as a graphic designer, which made me consider picking up drawing again. I attended several drawing programs at schools but I learned most from online resources. Now, I'm a freelance artist working on visual development. This means I design characters, props and backgrounds for games, animation and toys. However, you probably know me from my Instagram where I release tutorials and more. My goal is to create a place where people can learn the things I wanted to learn when I started out

HOW TO APPLY THIS BOOK .

In this book, I share everything I know from creating environments and working with perspective. Drawing environments is a useful skill to possess, because there is a lot of work to be found for environment artists. Of course, if your main passion is drawing characters you should pursue becoming a character designer. But if you want to work for the animation industry and look to increase your chances to become an artist at a studio, drawing environments is great. Even if you know you love drawing characters, it's really useful to at least have some understanding of how to draw environments .

In this book, I address different subjects. I start off with drawing perspective because that is your foundation for drawing environments. Later on, I will also go into drawing composition and more. The best way to improve your art is to keep drawing. This book contains exercises to help you practice. If you decide to do them, you can share them on your social media and tag me in it. I would love to see it and maybe I can give some feedback if you want.

Happy drawing and I hope you will enjoy the book.

Best,
Mitch Leeuwe

TABLE OF CONTENT

Drawing perspective 1

Understanding composition..27

Drawing props......... 50

Creating effects............ 60

Drawing backgrounds........ 63

Creating a portfolio piece....... 70

Drawing Perspective

Drawing perspective

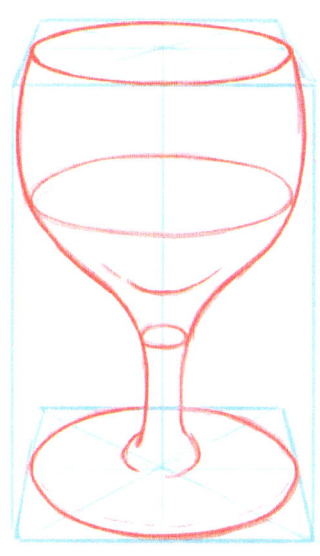

Perspective can be daunting. And it sometimes scares off people to startworking on environments. However, perspective is something you can learn and it doesn't have to be that hard to do, actually. So, I made a few tutorials to make it as simple aspossible.

Keep it simple in the beginning and work from there. Start off with drawing cubes. The big advantage ofhuman cities is that we tend to build everything in straight shapes, mainlycubes. That makes drawing cities in perspective really suitable to begin with. Drawing organic shapes, like characters or trees, are more difficult but you can build those shapes from cubes as well. I'll give a fewexamples of this later on. In the examples of drawing perspective, I give a number of steps to follow. Some of these stepswill be repeated because they are so important. The way to learn to draw is to draw a lot and do a lot of repetition. Learning to draw takes a lot of time and sometimes it can evenbe boring because of that. But all that practice will pay off eventually.

Maybe, when you start learning perspective your drawings mightlook a bit stiff. Don't worry, that's normal when you just start out with that. You'll get more experience and once you have more experience, your drawings will look more natural again. This is because in the beginning you really need to focus and think about the technique. Gradually, you'll do it more automatically and don't have to think so much about it anymore. You can also refer to this book again when you are stuck in a drawing and look up the guides to help you remember how to fix a perspective problem.

THE HORIZON

The horizon is the line where everything seems to end. When you're standing at a beach, you get a clear view of the horizon. The vanishing point is the point where all the lines disappear into. Like a road disappearing in the distance.

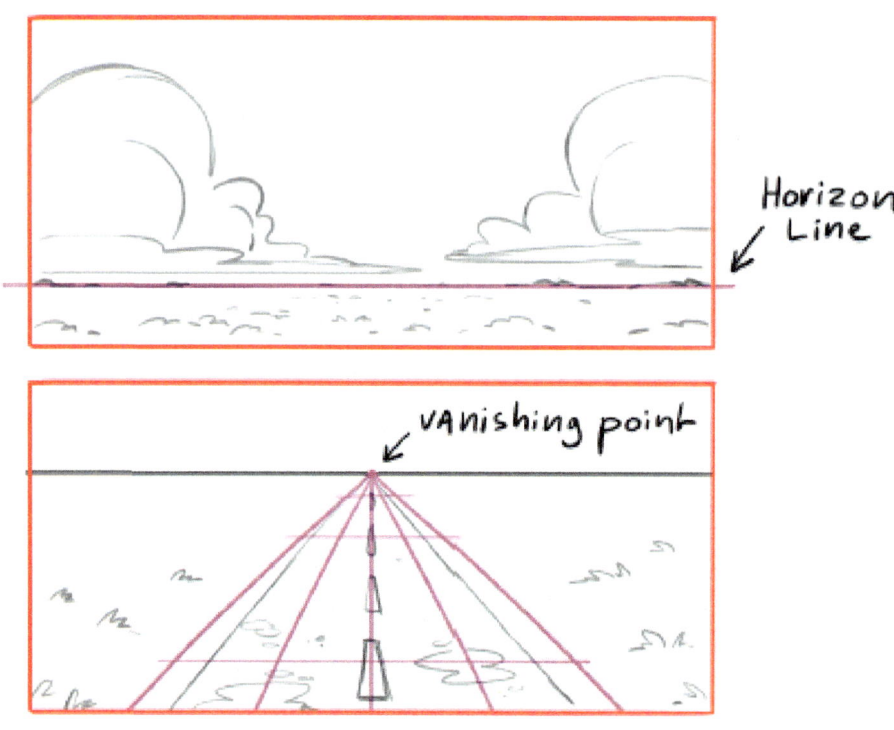

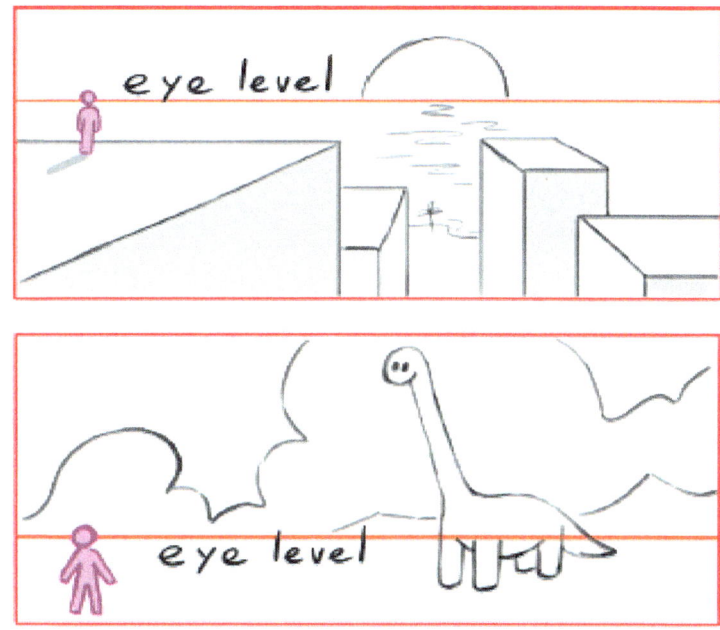

A horizon line is also called the eye level line. When you can see it, it's the separation between the sky or water

Foreshortening

Foreshortening. In this example you see a person lookingat a cylinder. When the cylinder is parallel, you don't see any foreshortening but when it's rotated 45 degrees, you'll see the foreshortening. The cylinder appears to be shorter.

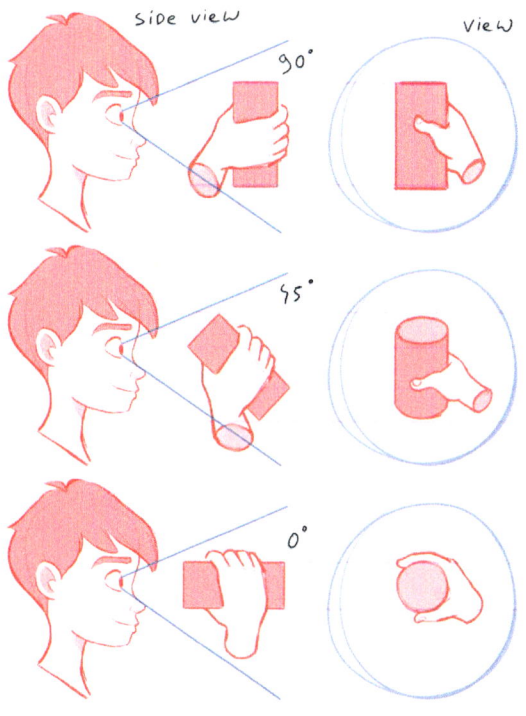

When you are looking at a wall and stand parallel to it, you'll see the wall as a flat plane. However, when you don't stand parallel to it, you'll see the top and bottom line of the wall coming together as they get closer to the horizon line.

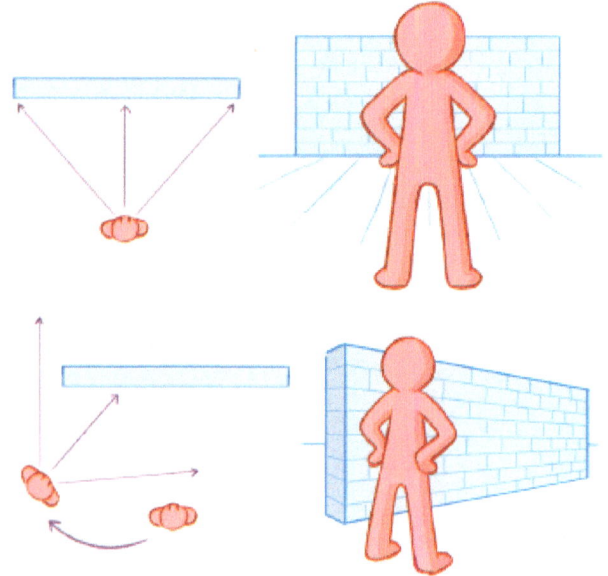

We see the world through our eyes. We call this area the 'cone of vision'. In the middle, there is the line of sight. Using this can help you understand what we see when we are looking at an object. Later I will talk about a floor plan and show more examples of this subject

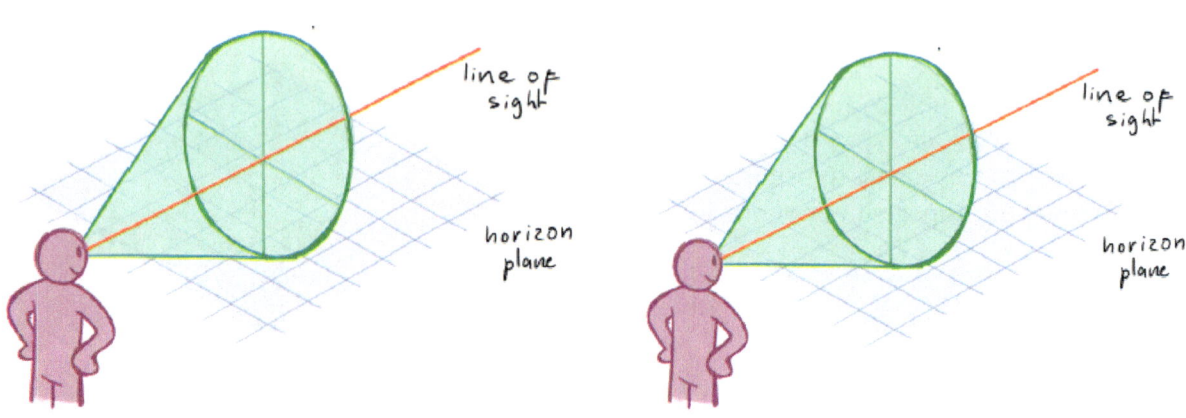

Point of view

In this example, we look at an object from different angles. So, the view from a higher angle will be different than a view from a low angle.

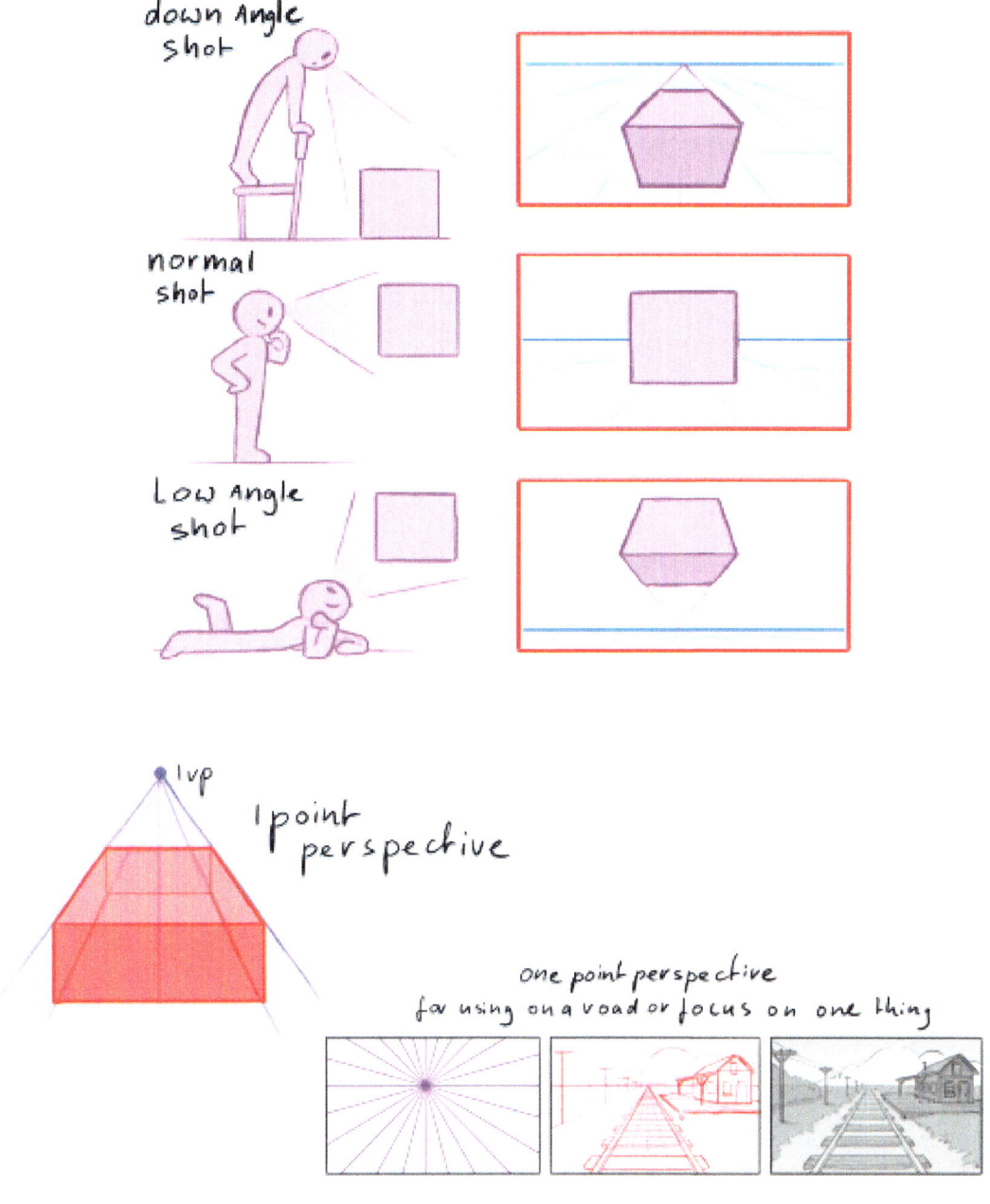

One-point perspective :

We talk about a one-point perspective when there is only one vanishing point (vp) on the horizon line. You'll come across this type of perspective when drawing roads, railway tracks, halls or buildings when directly facing the camera.

Two-point perspective :

When a drawing has two vanishing points we call this a two-point perspective. You can now draw the objects from the previous exercise in two-point perspective. The objects will look rotated. In the example you see the corner of the house.

Learn more!
Try to draw some objects in two-point perspective.

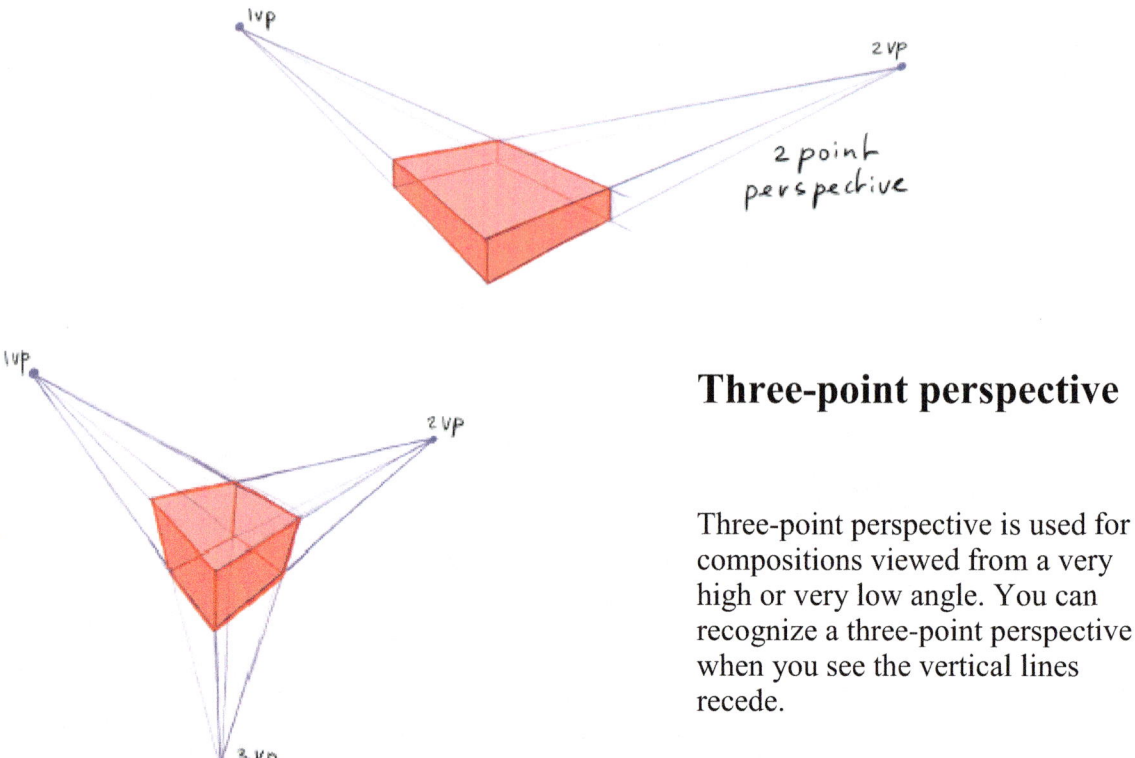

Three-point perspective

Three-point perspective is used for compositions viewed from a very high or very low angle. You can recognize a three-point perspective when you see the vertical lines recede.

Objects with different angles .

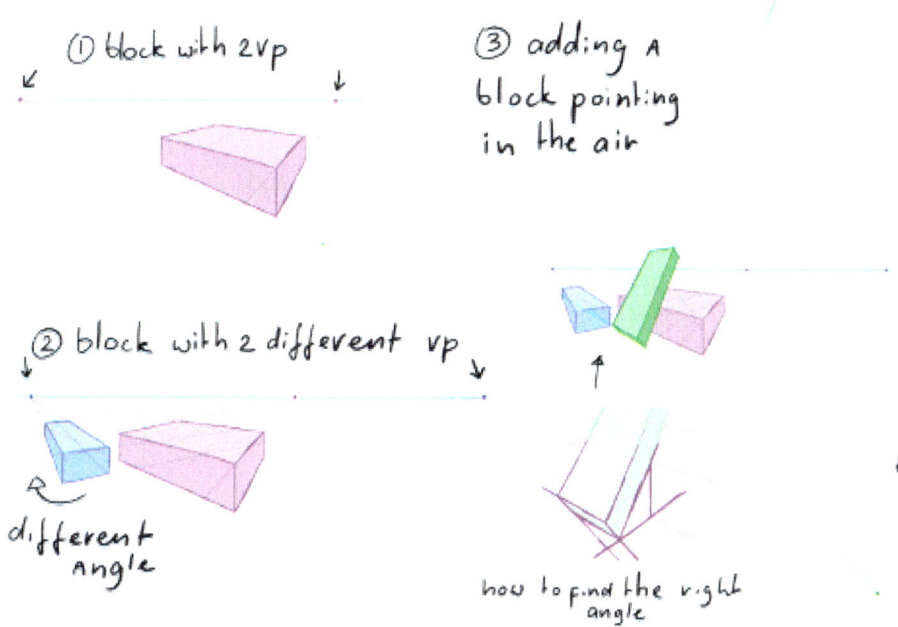

Not everything is at the same angle, oftentimes two objects have different angles. In this image I show how you can draw those objects. Most of the time, I guess how it's turned. Make a rough sketch and when it feels right, ad the vanishing points to the horizon line.

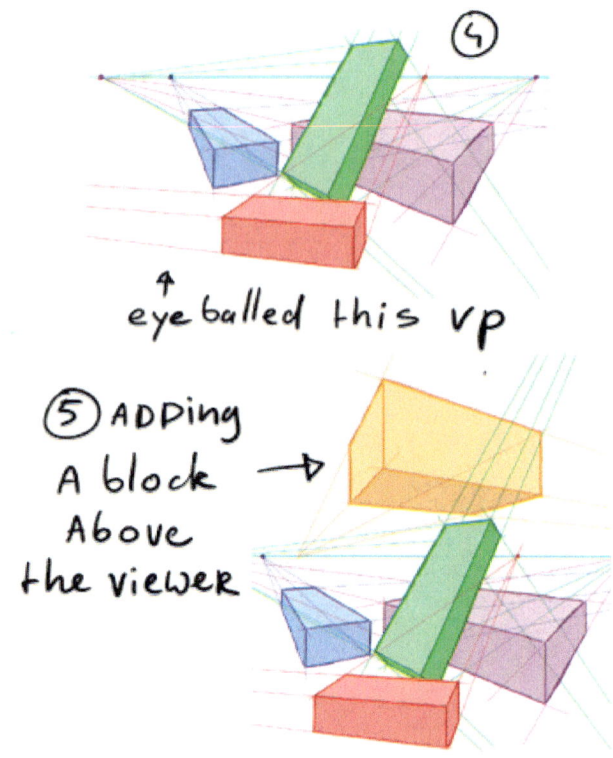

Distortion .

Here you can see all the three types of perspective next to each other. If you draw an object too far away from the vanishing point objects start to look too distorted and extreme.

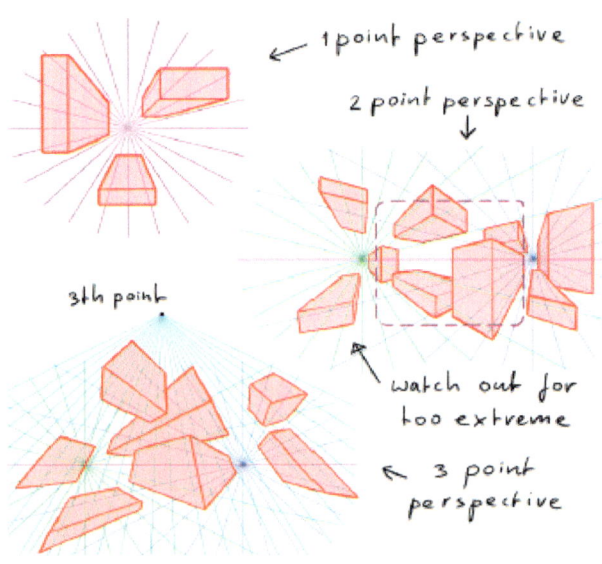

Draw a house .

Example of how to draw a house with a three-point perspective. The exaggerated third point gives it this cartoony feeling. Using big shapes first makes it way easier to draw. It's also a great way to determine the proportions before you start adding details. I added time to it, but when you're learning, you shouldn't focus too much on that.

First try to learn how to do it and once you get it, you can try doing it faster. You start with the horizon line. Add the vanishing points and after that you start adding the big shapes.

Draw a street .

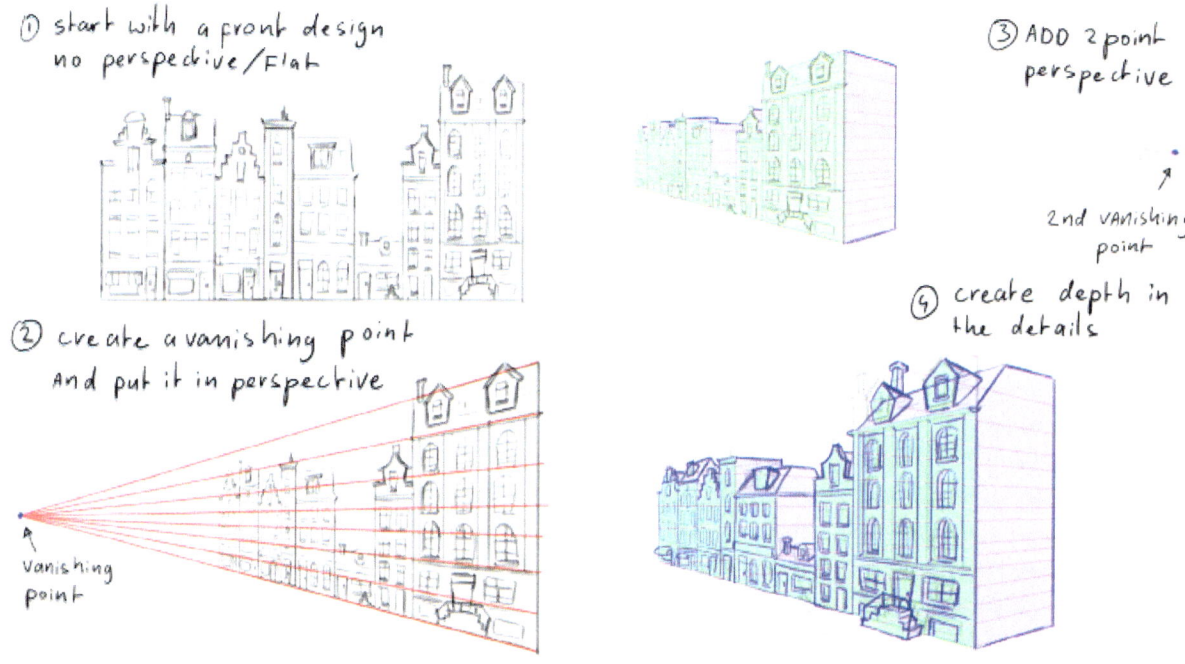

Drawing complex buildings can be tricky. Doing it this way makes it way easier. Of course, this method only works digitally. However, on paper it actually helps if you first draw the front view so you can use that as a reference when drawing it in perspective. This method also works great if you have to add paintings on a wall etc.

Place two perspective points based on rough sketch

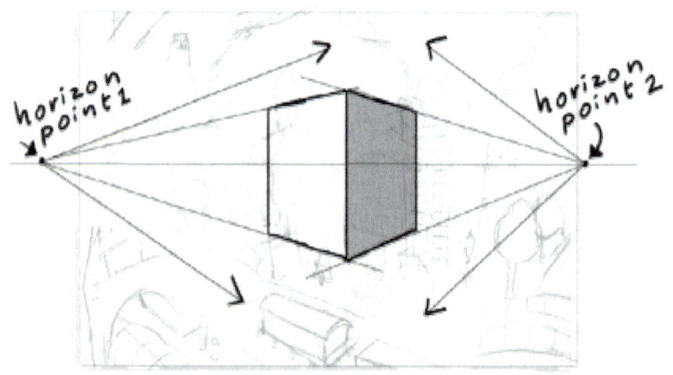

Make a grid of each point

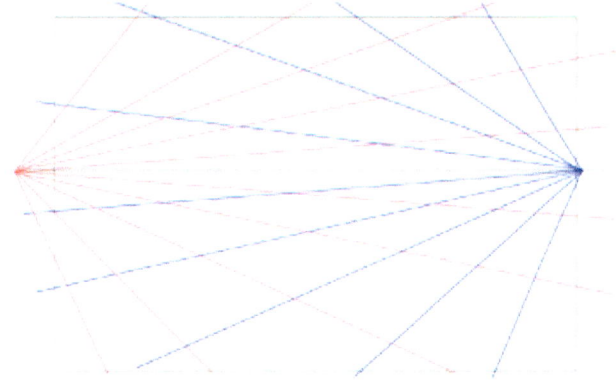

Here is a more classic way of drawing a street in two - point perspective. I often start with a rough sketch and after, I draw the perspective on top of that and make everything right. To be able to do a rough sketch, you need to have a good understanding of perspective.

Start sketching everything on the perspective grid

After that you can start working on the final line work

It's a good exercise to also learn to quickly sketch an environment in perspective. And once you have a rough sketch you like, you can start adding all the perspective lines and make it work .

Off page vanishing points

In some cases, there isn't a lot of space on the page to create all the vanishing points. This is a handy method to create vanishing points without creating an enormously long horizon and far away vanishing points.

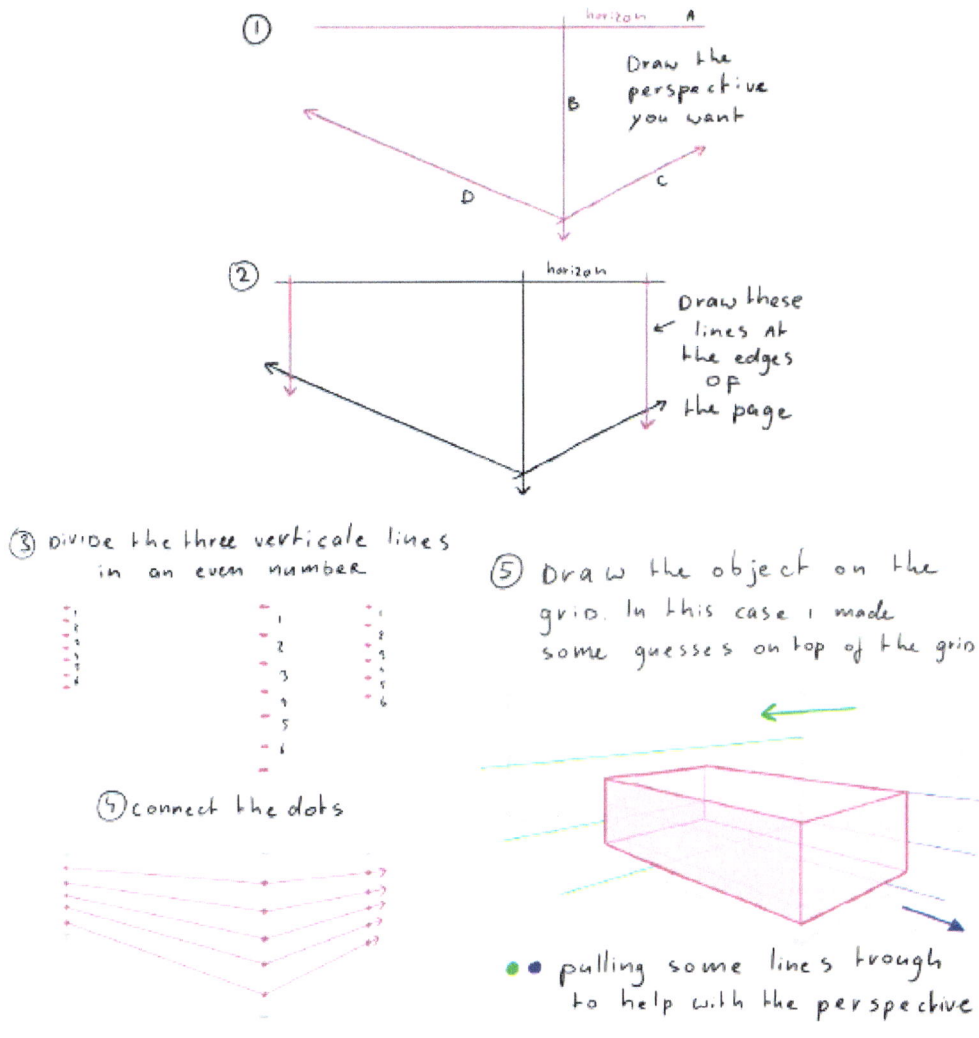

Row of lanterns

This is a useful trick I often use to calculate the distance between objects. It's ideal to create a repeating pattern in perspective, like these lamp posts. You can also use it for buildings or a fence. This trick works vertically, as well. For example, for floors of a building.

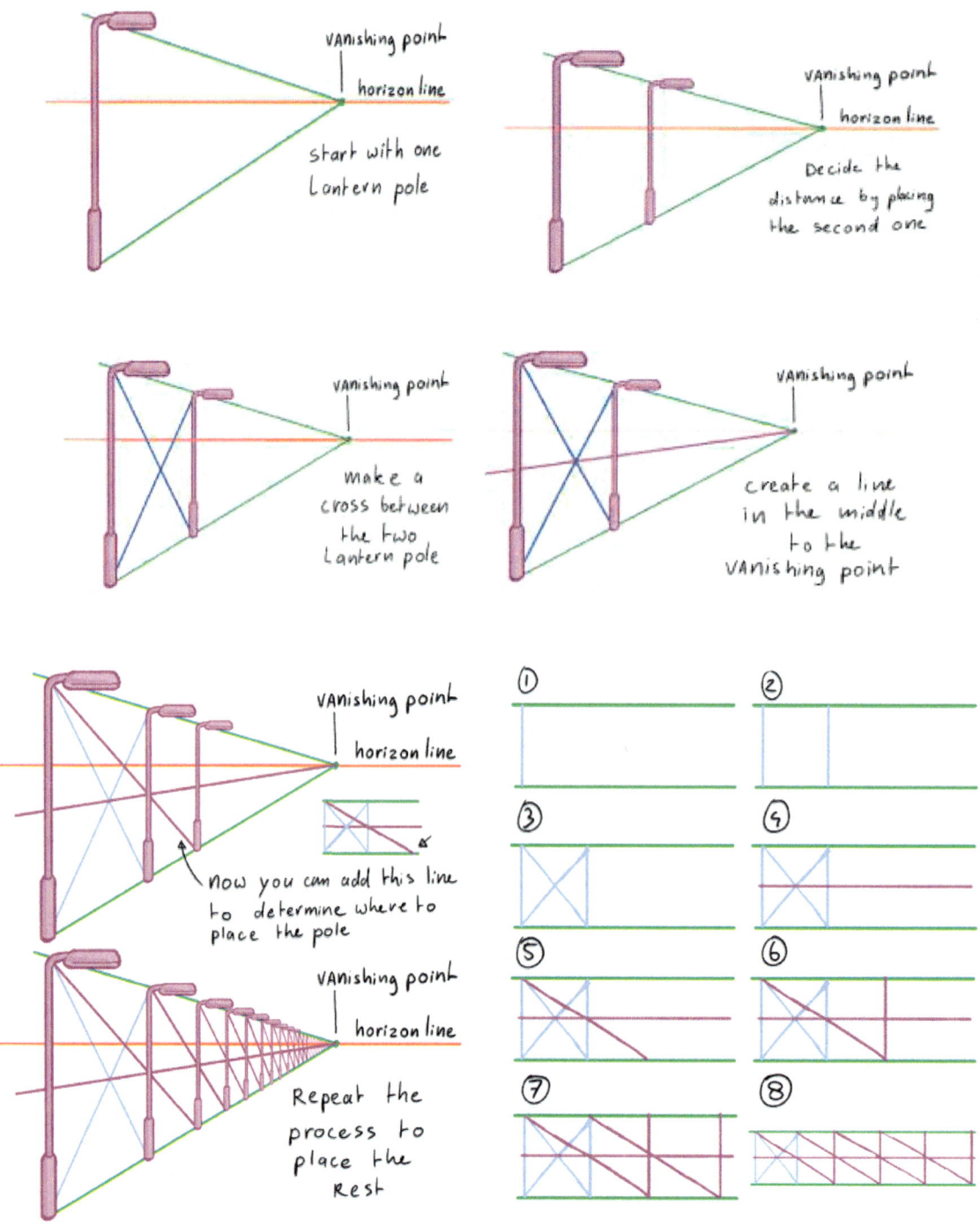

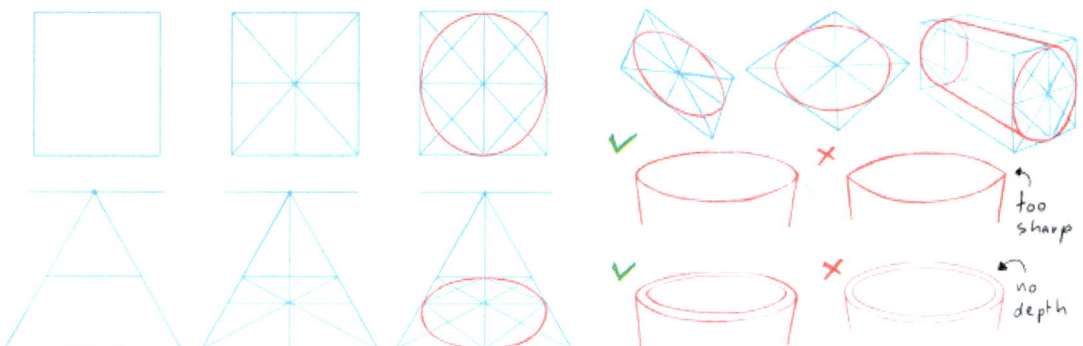

A CIRCLE IN PERSPECTIVE

Drawing circles in perspective can be quite hard. However, there is a way to calculate all points of a circle. This makes it a lot easier to figure out how distortion changes the shape.

It's really useful to practice this a lot because that way you can develop a feeling for it and it will get easier .

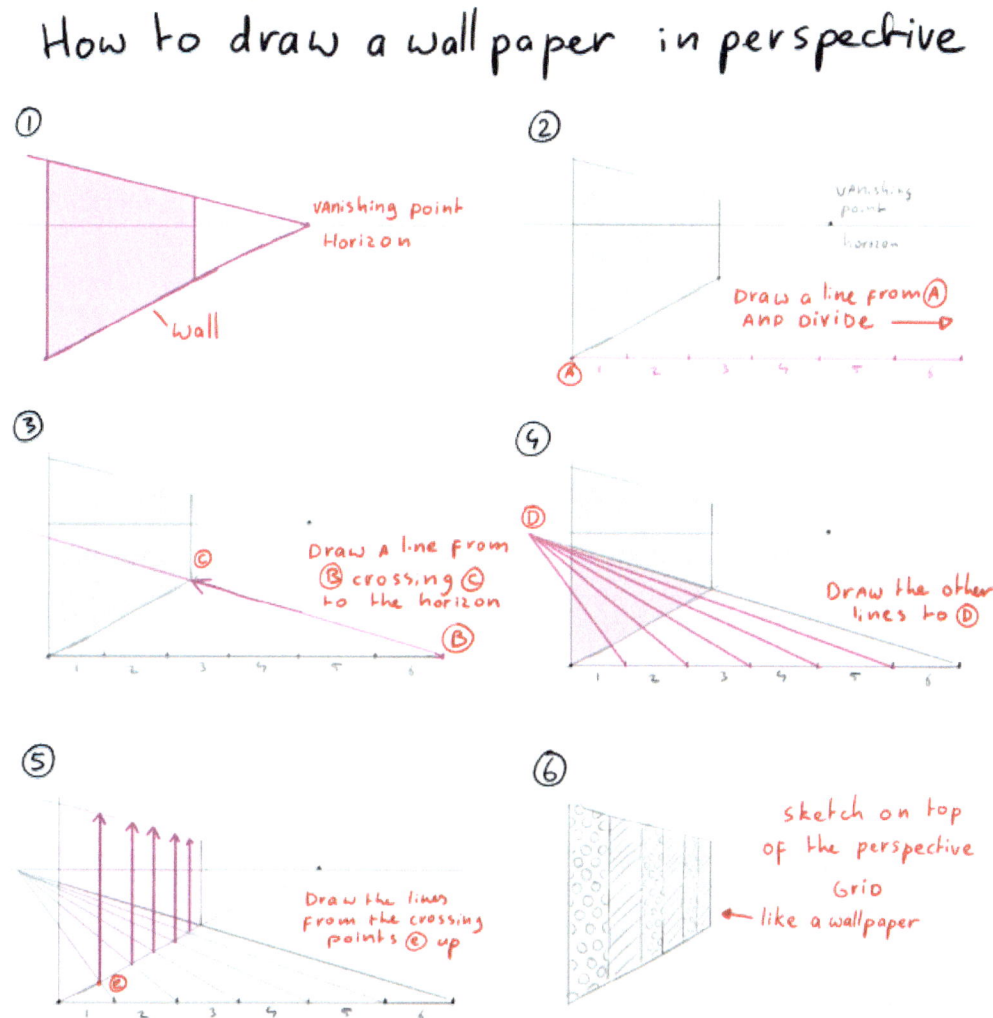

DIVIDE A WALL IN EVEN PARTS

There are multiple ways to figure out what the size of a column should be. This is very useful because you can determine beforehand how many rows you want to make .

DRAW A TILED FLOOR

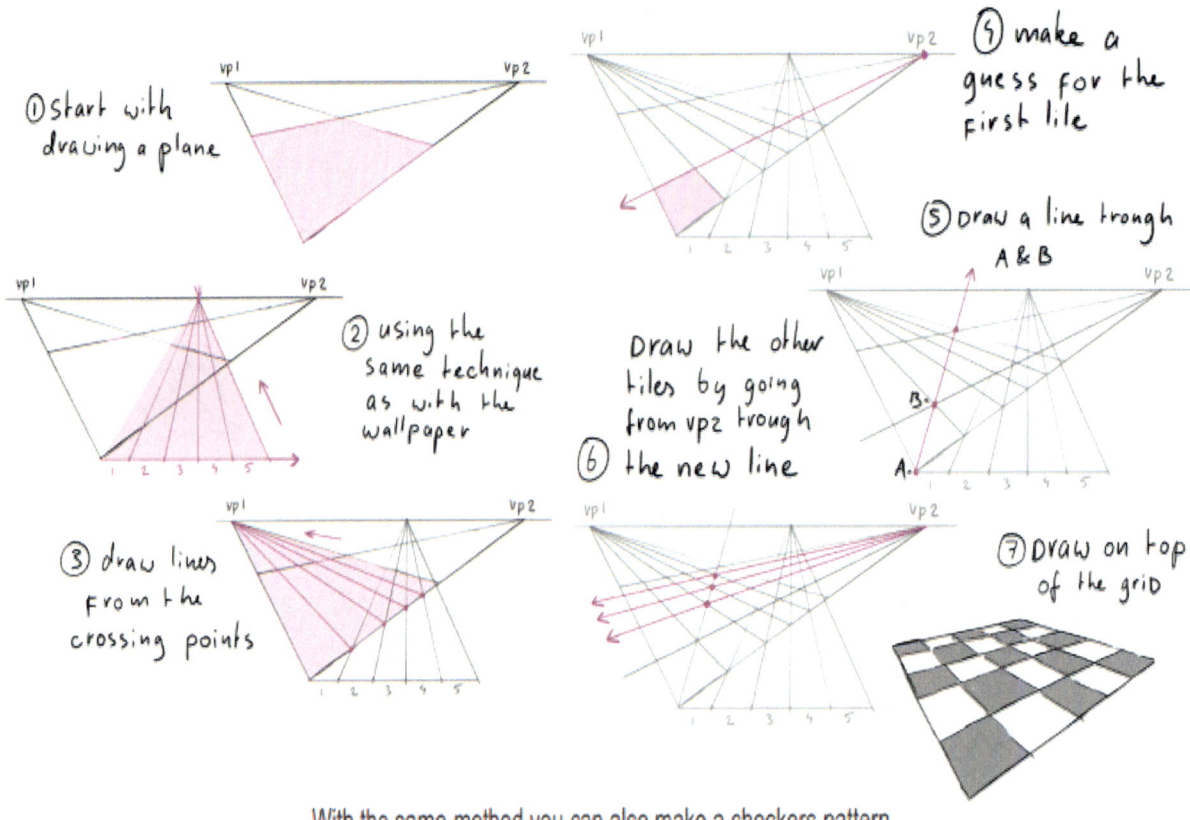

With the same method you can also make a checkers pattern.

Drawing a roof

Usually, I draw roofs freehand because most of the time, it works if those lines are parallel. But with this trick you can quickly get the roof right .

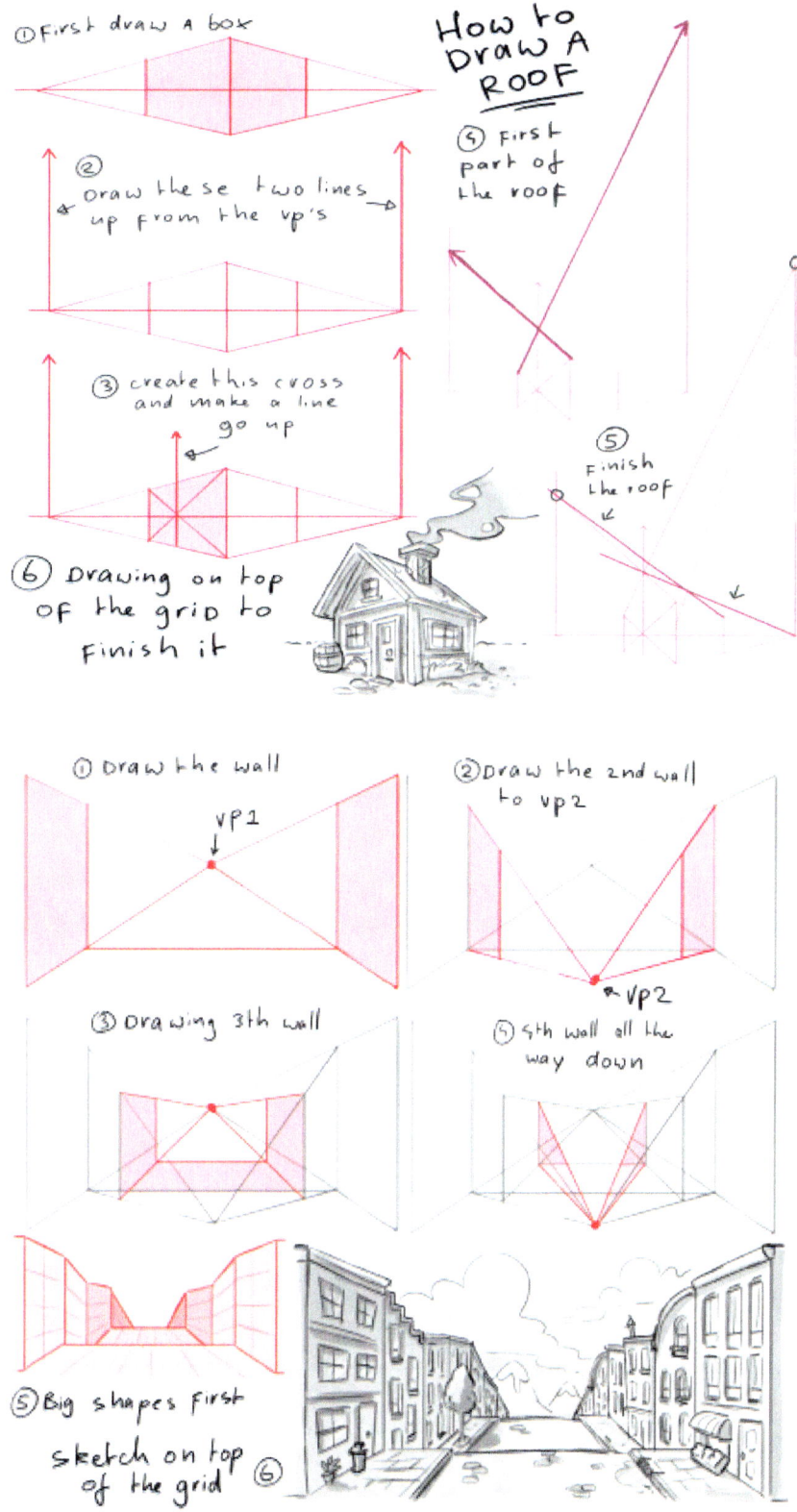

A downhill street

Drawing a street cascading downward is a great way of making an interesting composition. Drawing it in these steps will make it easier to do. Notice that it's still a one-point perspective.

Multipoint perspective

Most people see the world through two eyes. When you look at something and you switch between your left and right eye, you can see their vanishing points are slightly different. You can use this technique to add a bit more depth to your drawing.

Because the two eyes both have a different vanishing point, we see depth. That's also the purpose of those blue
and red glasses you see at old 3D theatres.

DRAW A pyramid

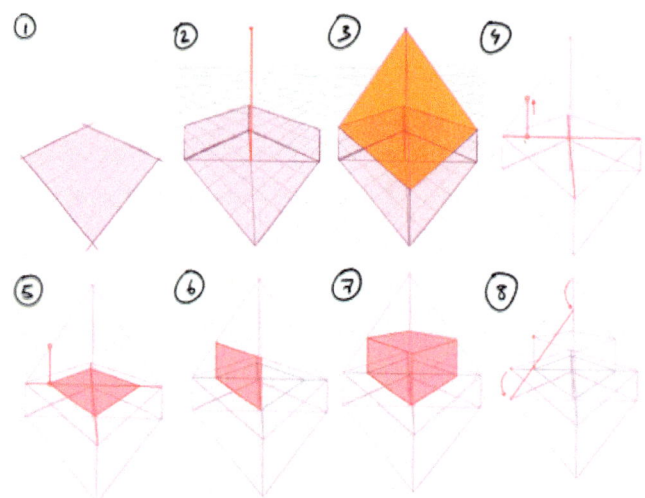

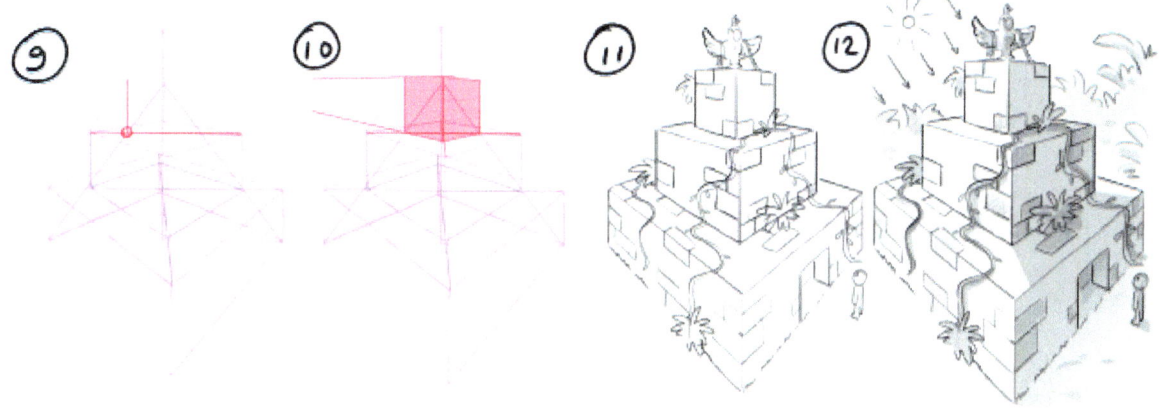

This method is useful when you're drawing a pyramid or anything that consists of smaller blocks stacked on top of bigger ones. Like a pile of clothes, birthday cake or kids' wooden play bocks.

DRAW A banana pan

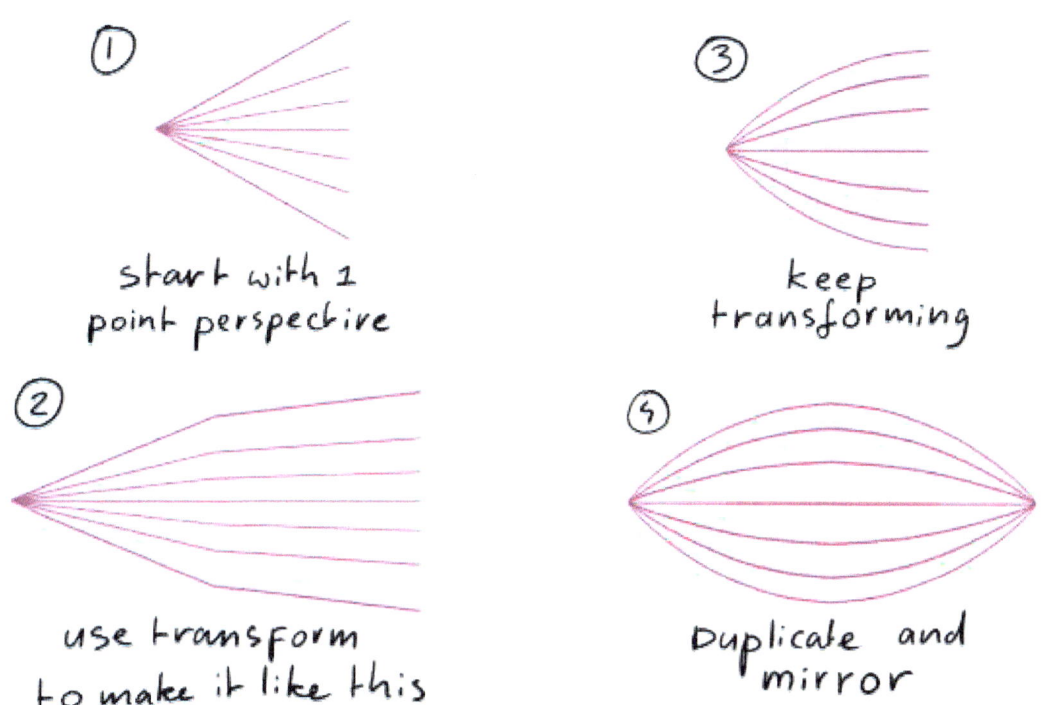

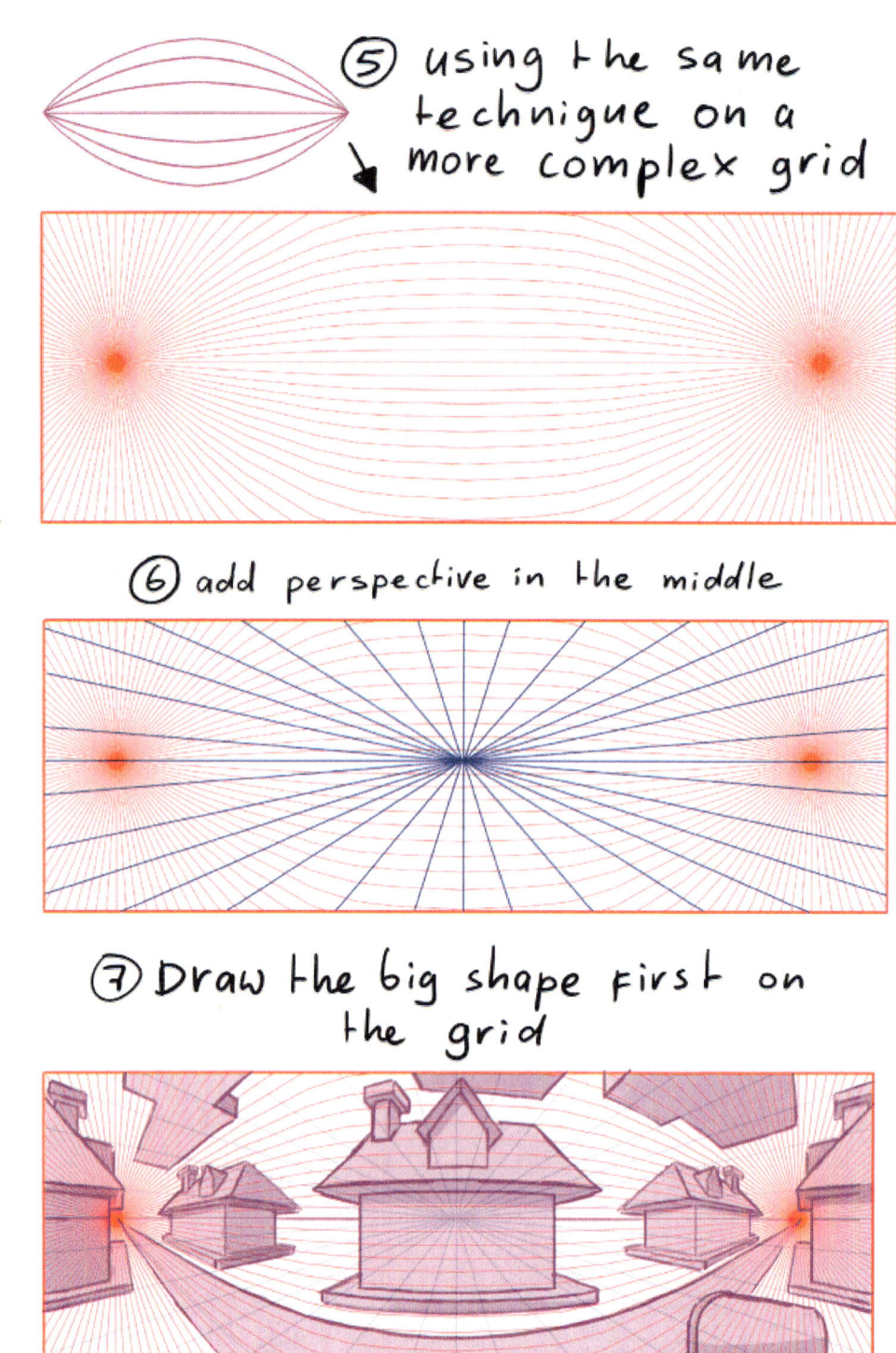

This is called a banana pan. These kinds of backgrounds are often used for a horizontal pan. A pan is when the camera horizontally moves from one . point to another (I'll explain more later about camera movement)

⑧ sketch on top of those shapes and add shadow

Spherical perspective.

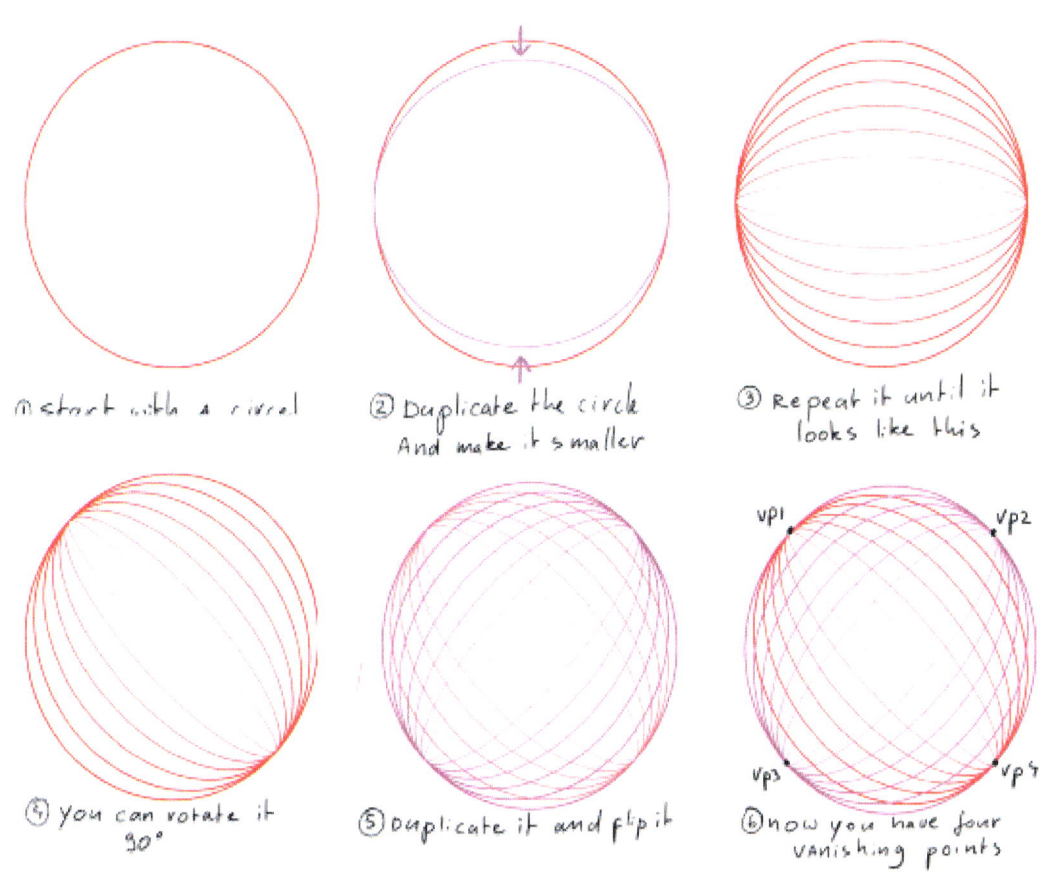

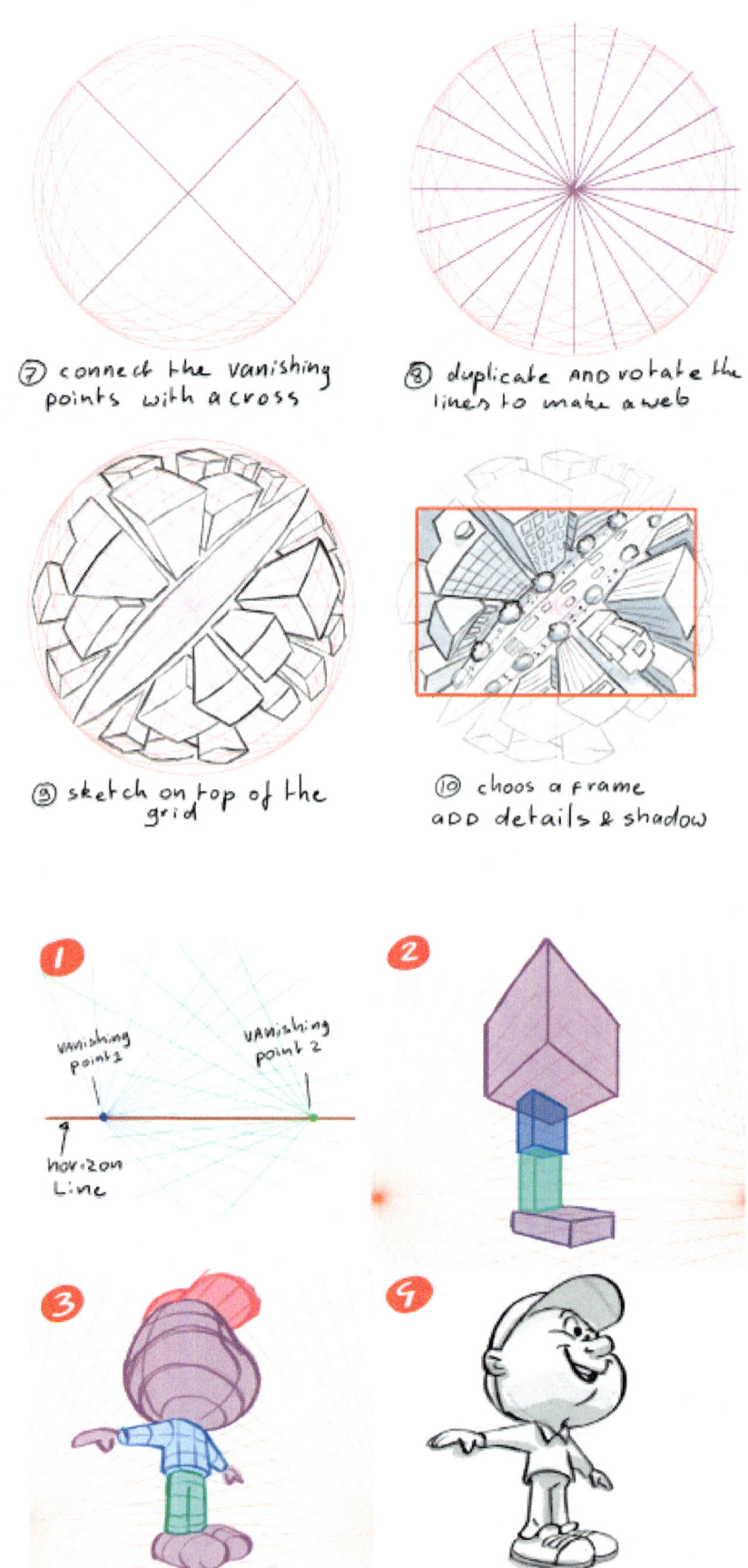

Characters in perspective .

Steps of drawing a character. I first draw cubes so I can then draw bodies and other organic shapes inside those cubes. Cubes are easy shapes to draw in perspective.

Characters in perspective on a background

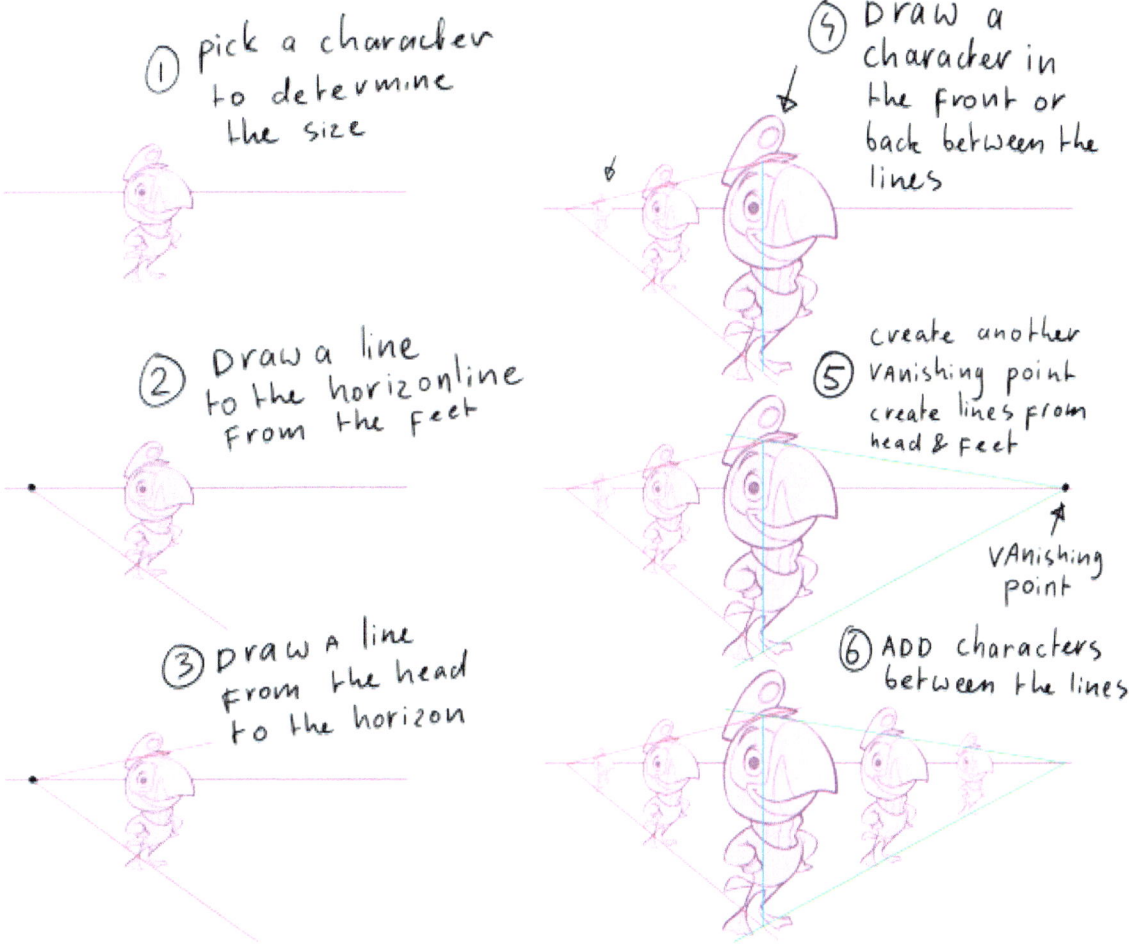

Drawing characters in perspective is basically the same as drawing objects. To make it easier, I start by drawing blocks and then draw the more organic shapes inside of them. For drawing characters, I use cubes, cylinders and spheres.

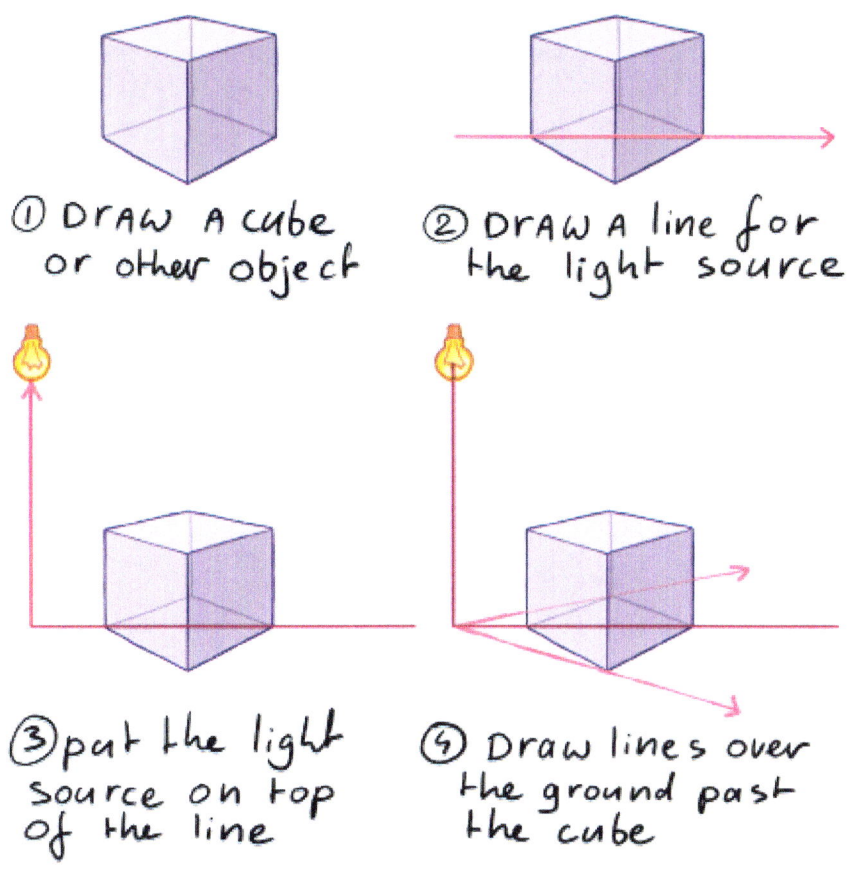

Shadows in perspective.

If you want to draw a shadow that matches the perspective, these steps will guide you to where the shadow lands.
You can also apply this with organic shapes. For organic shapes you have to draw more guidelines intersecting the edges of the object and touching the ground. I usually draw a few lines like this and then I make an estimation and fill in the gaps.

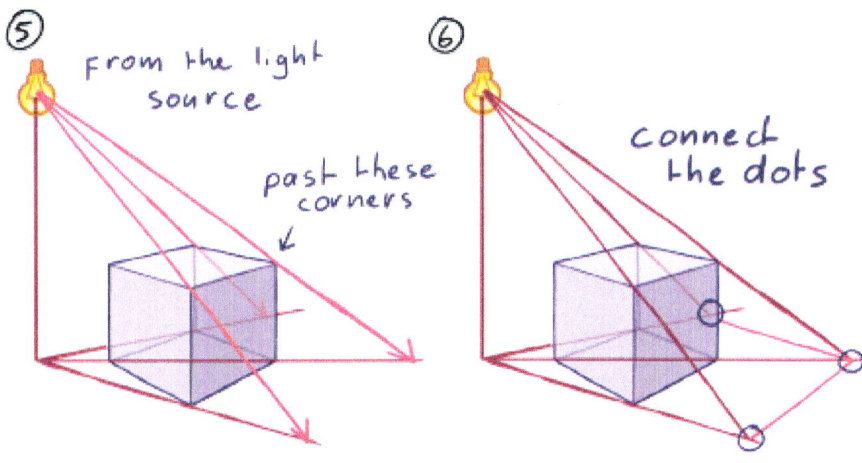

Remember that the shadow always follows the shape of the object, like in these examples.

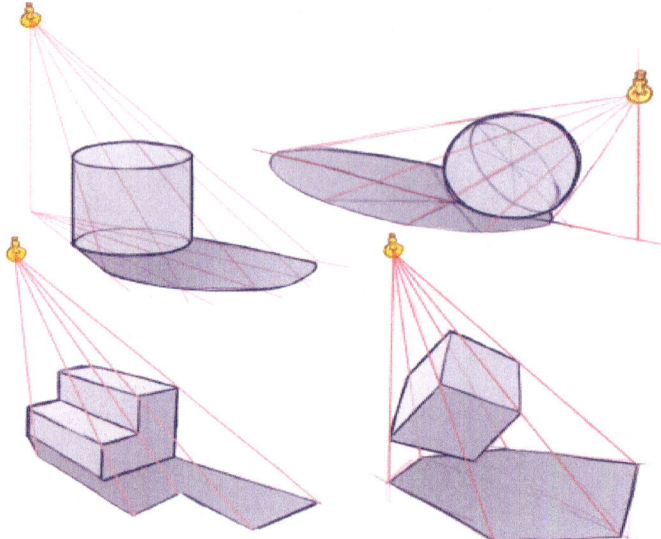

Here you can see how the lighting is used on an object like this. Basically, is works the same as with a cube. Of course, you can go as accurate as you want with it. Normally, I only apply it to the big shapes and make educated guesses for the smaller shapes.

Understanding Composition

no clear composition don't know where to look

clear composition you can see what is happening

Composition .

Composition is the placement or arrangement of visual elements in a scene, drawing or illustration. It is an organization of different elements which all serve to tell the story .

Composition means "putting together" and with composition you can guide the eye and make sense of a drawing. Without composition we wouldn't know where to look.

The example on the left page shows the difference between an unclear composition and a clean composition. In the unclear example, all the elements are scattered around the image without guiding the viewer's eye to a certain point. In the example with the clear composition, the story is clear in a split second; two persons saying hi to each other. In this part of the book I'll give you tips and tools to create clear compositions your self.

Ascpect ratio

When you start making a drawing, it's important to first think about what screen aspect ratio you want to use. This is the horizonal width of a screen (TV, cinema, computer etc.) in relation to it's vertical height.
In this example you see the most used screens. Of course, you have even more options, like phones and tablets. Each aspect ratio has its own rules for compositions and camera movements.

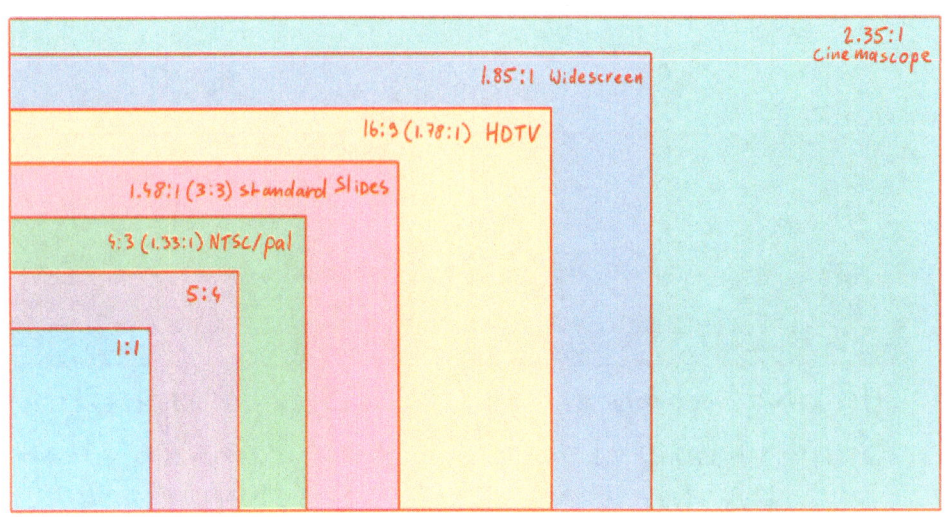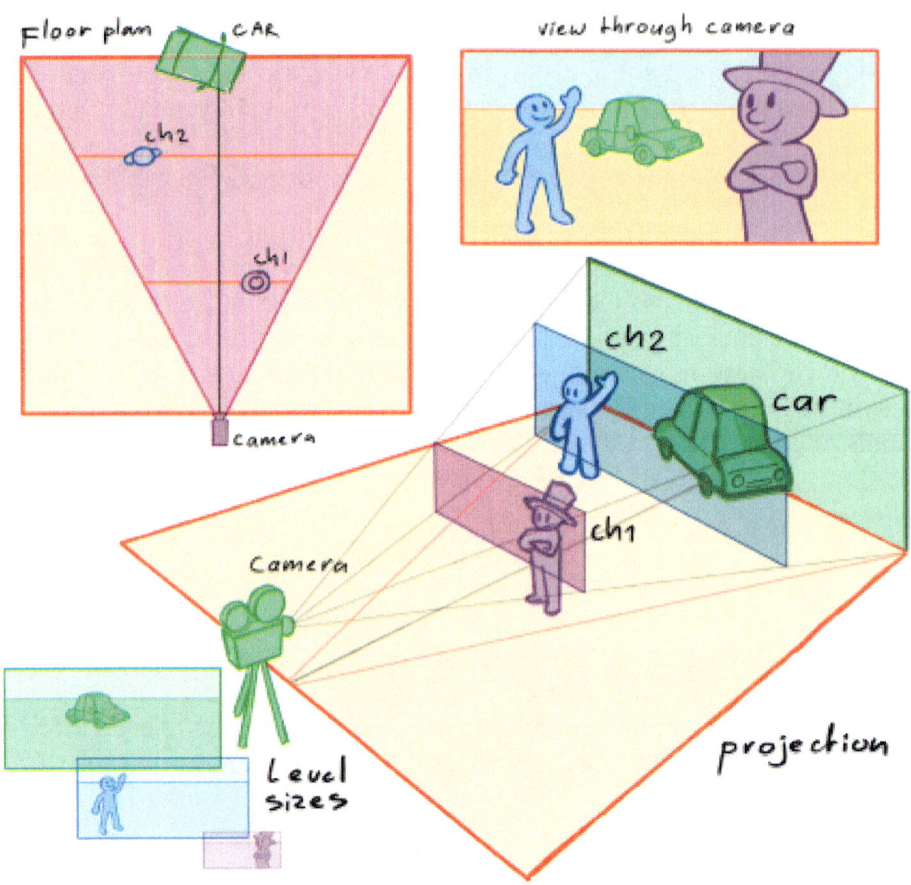

SET UP A COMPOSITON

Complex compositions can be hard to draw. Using a stage plan is a nice trick to figure out how to draw different angles.

So, when I draw, I often start with a floor plan. Then, I break it all down and plan it out before I start on the actual drawing. When you draw something like this out on paper you also see how perspective works; why it is that someone in the distance is smaller on screen than someone standing in front .

CAMERA SHOTS

Think on what kind of shots you want to use. In a good movie every shot is made with a certain idea behind it. For example, extreme close-up shots aren't used that often. But you can use it when you want to make an emotional impact .

Normal shots are very commonly used for characters, it's neutral. But if we want to let the viewer feel weaker or like a child, we can use a low angle (also called frog perspective). If we want to let the viewer feel powerful and mighty we can use a high angle, also called a bird view.

SHOT TYPES

There are different types of shots and each type of shot lends itself for its own reason. The 'establishing shot' helps to establish a location, for example at the beginning of a movie. The 'over the shoulder' and the 'two shot' are perfect for conversations or conflict. The 'point of view' means that you are looking through the eyes of the character, for example when it's looking through a binocular. A 'Dutch angle' can be used to make something feel strange or extra dynamic.

LESES

Using different lenses will give different effects. So, think about what story you want to tell and choose a lens accordingly. The smaller the lens, the wider your picture. The wider your lens, the narrower your picture. Our eyes are like a normal lens, this is how we perceive the world around us. When you use a wide-angle lens, everything seems really big and distorted. You can use this when you want something to feel really impressive. A telescope lens will give a very flat perspective. The object that it is focused on is the only sharp object in the shot, the rest is out of focus. This is often used when we want to give the viewer the impression that someone is observing from a great distance. Like a sniper, stalker, lion etc.

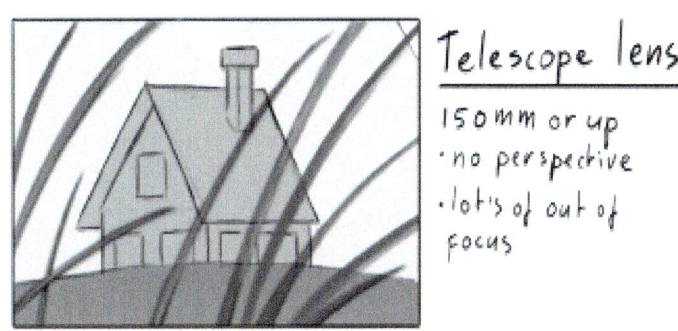

CAMERA MOVEMENT .

Cameras can move during filming. Each type of camera movement has a different effect on how the story is experienced by your audience.

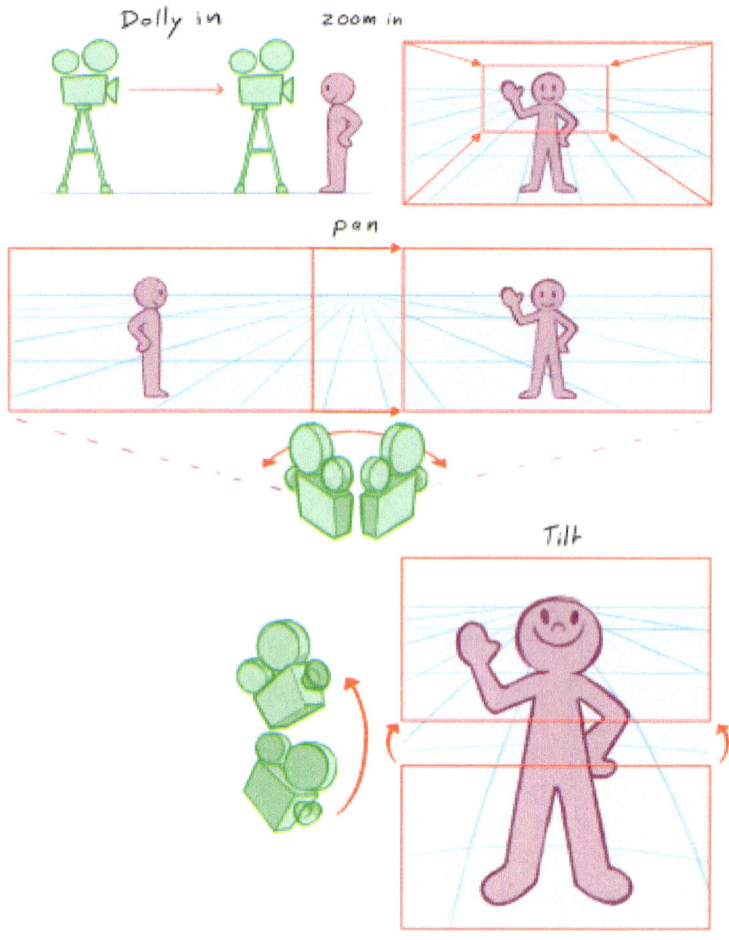

First, have a 'zoom in'. Actually, we call it a zoom in when the lens literally zooms in. We refer to a 'dolly in' when we move the camera towards an object.

We call something a 'pan' when we move the camera horizontally, these shots are great when you are following something or when you want to reveal something. A 'tilt' can be used when you want to make something dramatic. Maybe someone has fallen and first looks at the feet and then starts to look up to see who made him fall .

180° rule

In filmmaking, there are a lot of rules. And of course, rules can be broken. The 180-degree rule is a guideline for the spatial relationship between the characters and objects in a scene. When you follow this 'rule', you keep the camera on one side of an imaginary axis between two characters, the first character is always first in the frame. This way you avoid confusion about the position of the characters and objects in the scene.

Composition basics .

Try to avoid the middle unless you do it on purpose. In some movies, the director deliberately chooses to do this. But when you avoid the middle, you will get a more interesting composition that feels more natural.

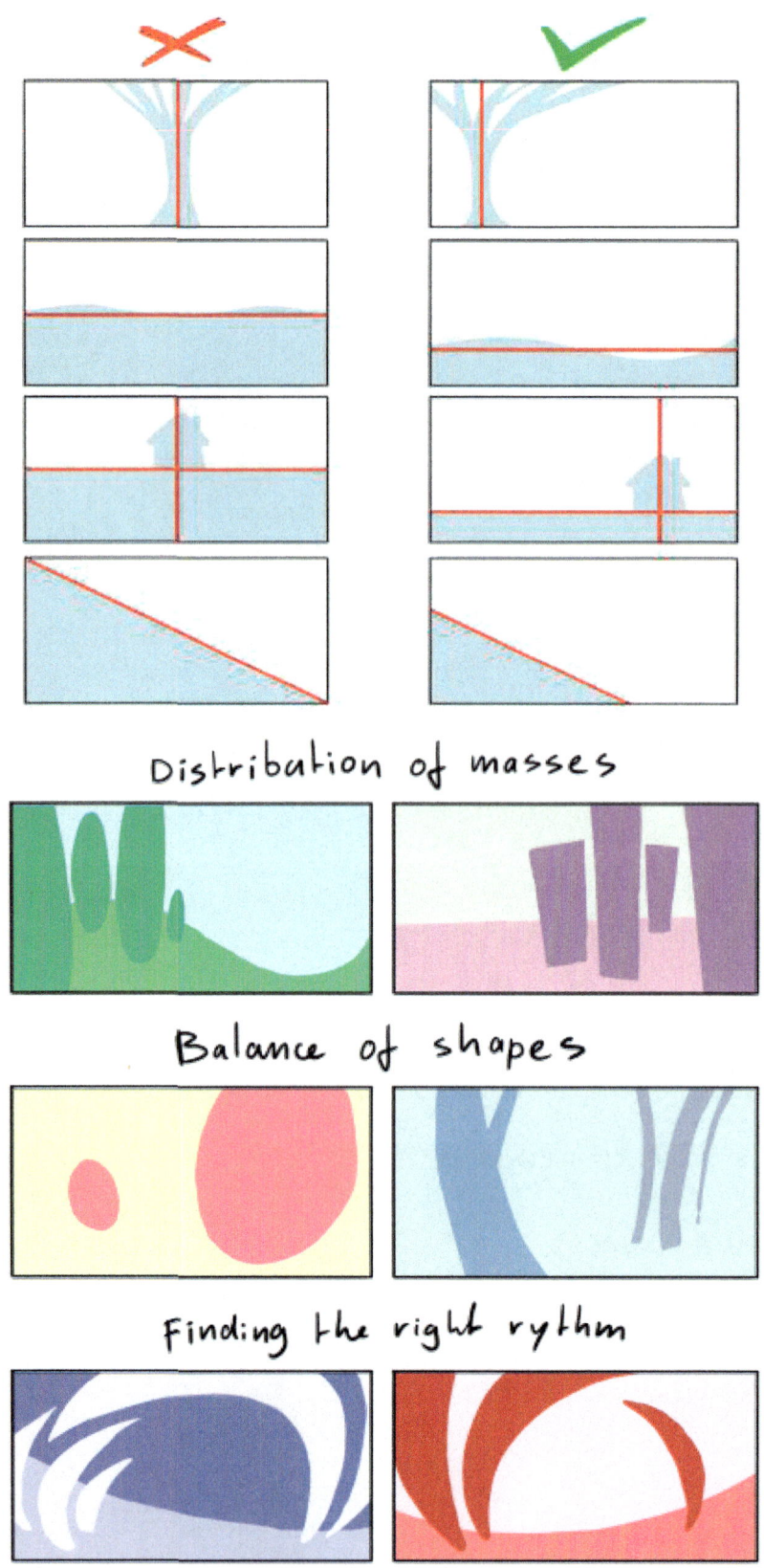

With these examples I tried to find rhythm and an interesting composition. Again, composition is about guiding the viewer's eye into a specific direction.

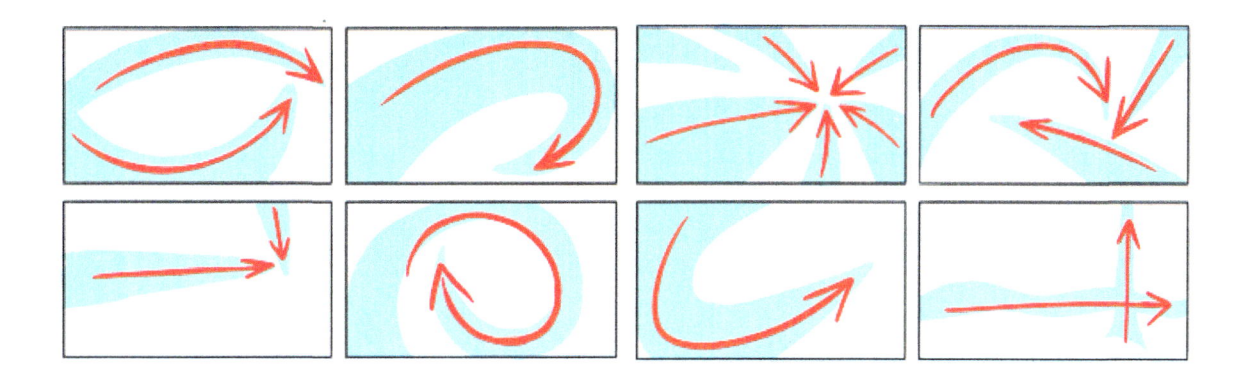

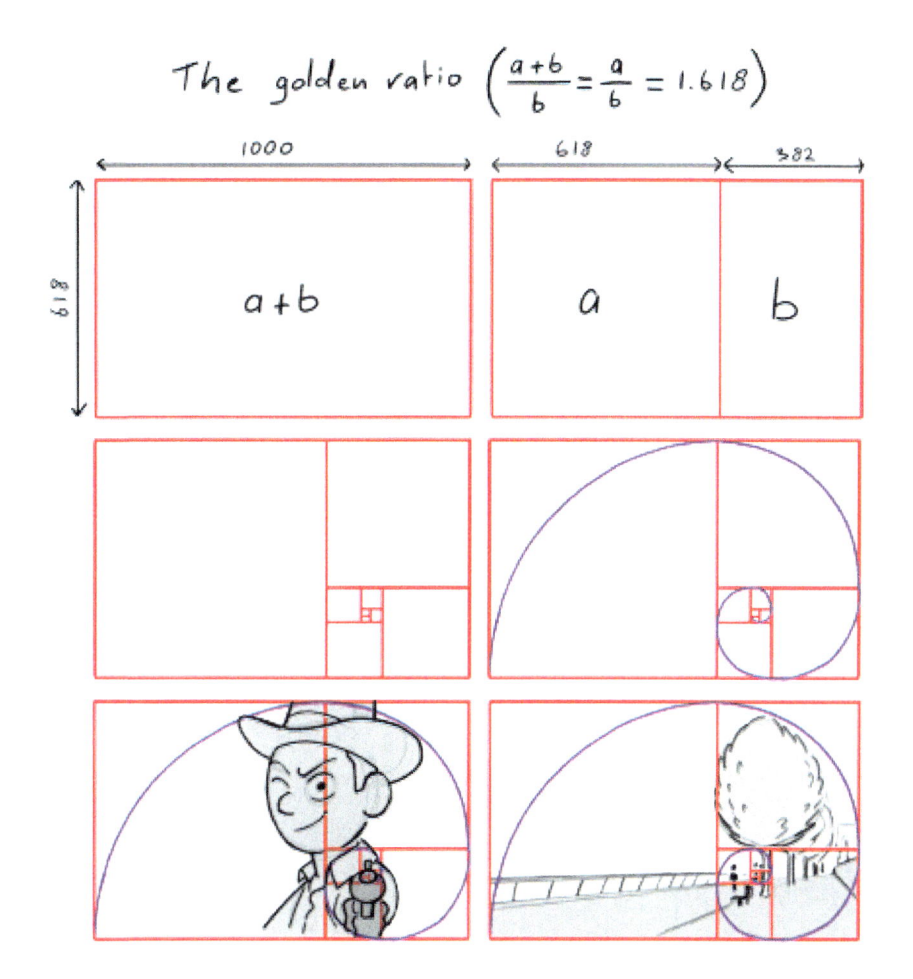

THE GOLDEN RATIO

The 'golden ratio' is the number 1.618. It is also called the 'golden mean' or 'golden section'. In the given example, you can see that if a+b is 1000, a is 618 and b is 382. If you keep dividing the square you get a spiral. In the twentieth century, artists and architects started to use the golden ratio, believing that the golden ratio is aesthetically pleasing.

RULE OF THIRDS AND RABATMENT

The rule of thirds' and 'rabatment' are basically simplifications of the golden ratio. But they do work and help you to avoid the middle. With the rule of thirds, you divide the canvas into thirds, and you put the points of interest on the intersections (red grid). When you divide the grid again (purple lines), you can use these intersections or divide it once more (green grid) to have more intersection points to use.

Rabatment is a way to make a composition by dividing the canvas into squares and use that to guide your drawing. With this technique you can also use the intersection points to place the points of interest.

COMPOSITION EXAMPLES

Here are some examples of compositions from movies. Pausing a movie and looking for the composition is a great exercise to improve your own eye for composition.

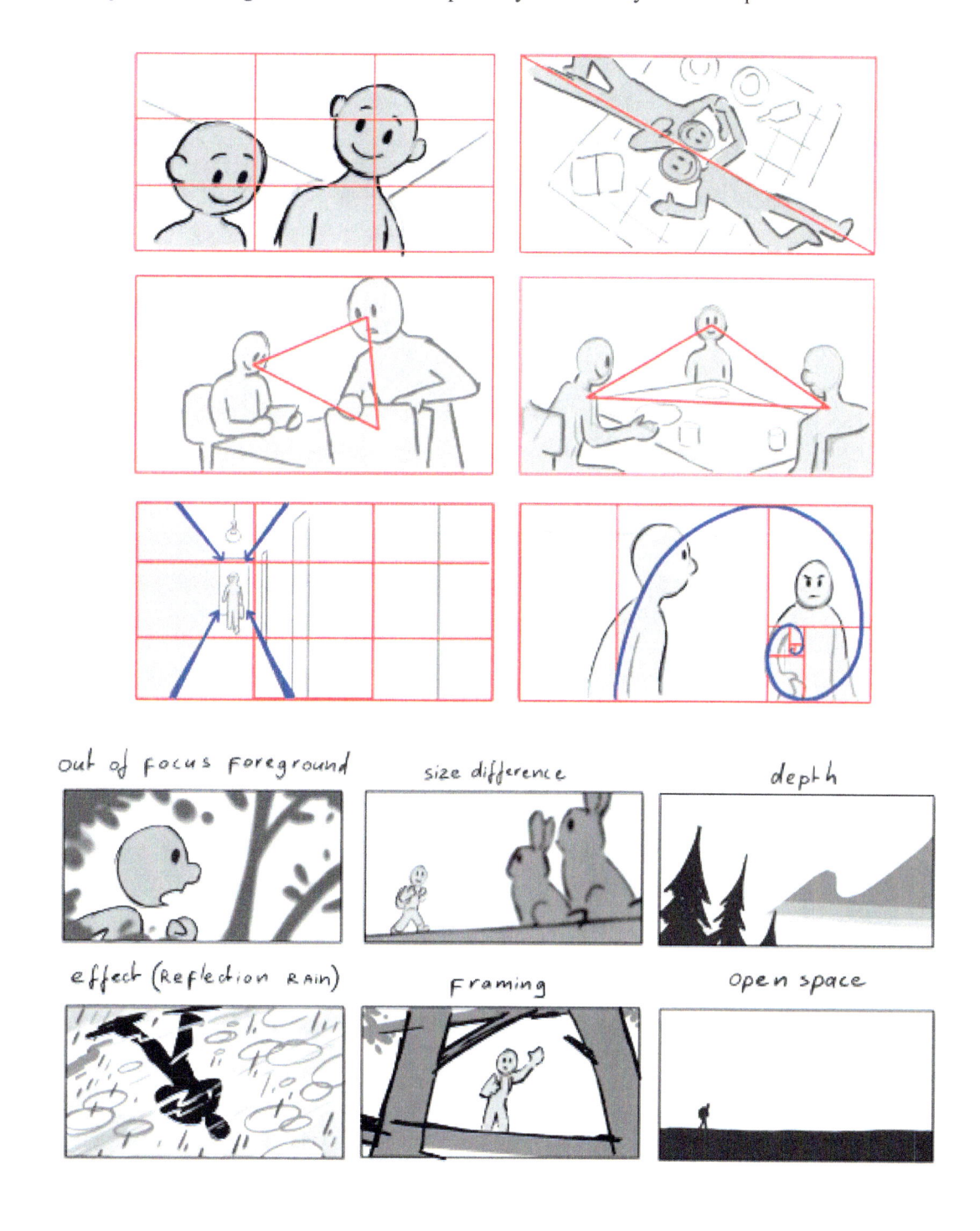

out of focus foreground

size difference

depth

effect (Reflection Rain)

Framing

open space

LEADING EYE

Apart from using the golden ratio, you can also use other ways to lead the eye. Like out of focus, size difference, depth, framing, open space, effects and more. Think about what is interesting for your composition and what you want to tell. Ask yourself: What fits and maybe even improves the way I tell my story?

The best way to learn this is to try it and observe and study movies. Try to see in movies what they want to tell and how they do that in a shot.

Positive & negative space

Positive and negative space are important parts of the composition. It's important to understand because it's one of the strongest tools for composition you have. With positive space, we mean objects, characters or area of interest. Negative space is the area around the objects, characters or area of interest.

With a certain balance between positive and negative space you can create different meanings, emotions and experiences. For example: The characters in the first image feels quite lonely or free because of the large negative space around him.

The power of three

In compositions 'three' makes everything better than two.

A composition of two tonal values can be very powerful. However, at the same time it can be limiting. A composition of three tonal values already gives way more options. The power of three also translates very well to the use of shapes, sizes and volumes.

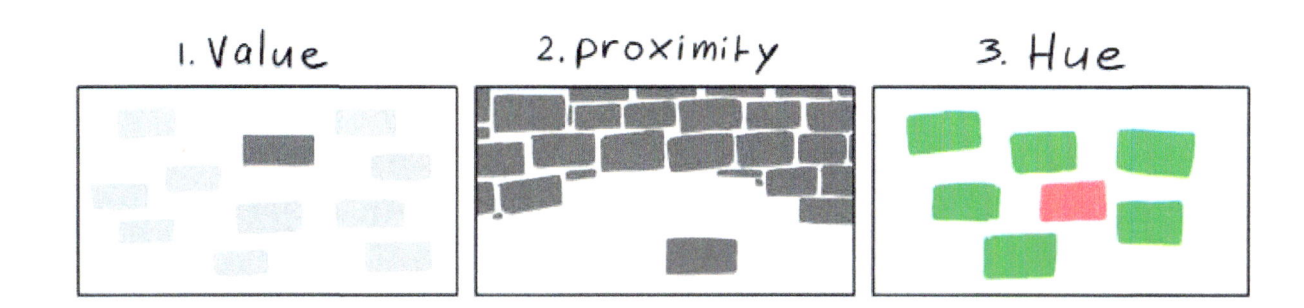

Contrast

Contrast is important in art. It's one of the principles that is used to distinguish one object from another.

If you manage to use contrast in a strong way, you can draw the attention to anything you want. You don't want everything to scream. You want the most important subject in your composition to stand out, you can do that by using one or more of the types of contrast mentioned in the examples on these pages. Value (1) is the strongest and texture is the most subtle (9)

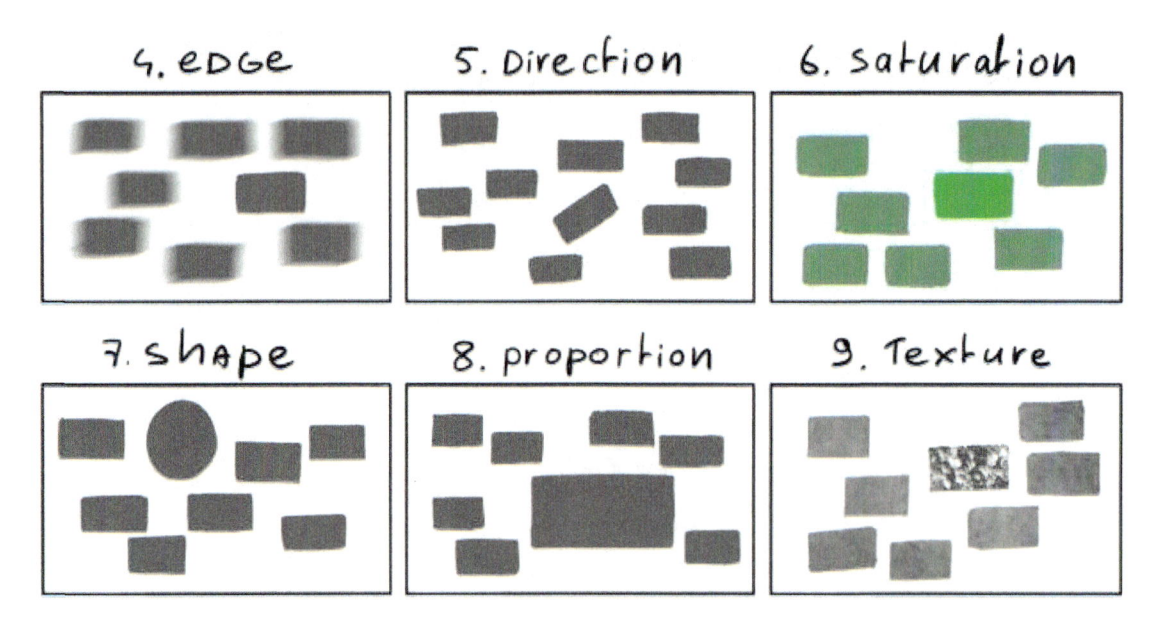

4. Edge 5. Direction 6. Saturation

7. Shape 8. Proportion 9. Texture

Reading direction

We Read from
Left → right
up ↓ down

Going towards   Going back

In most countries, we read from left to right. We are most comfortable with that. Because we are so used to reading from left to right, it influences what we expect to see in movies and illustrations. When a person walks into a scene and walks to the right, we expect to see this left to right movement in the next shot. It will be confusing otherwise.

You can choose to let your character move from right to left, but that will communicate that the character has forgotten something, or something like that, and is going back.

using A Horizontal pan

I'm going to work

I forgot my keys need to get back

using A vertical pan

Going to get some food

getting back with food

✓ space to move

✗ too close to the border

When framing the movement an object or character, it's important that the character has space to move in the direction that it is moving.

41

Tangents

Tangents occur when points connect to each other. A lot of people tend to connect lines on outline points, but that could make a wrong image and can be confusing. Try to overlap or separate the lines.

Foreshortening

When drawing backgrounds, try to use as much foreshortening as possible, so there will be more depth in the drawing. Of course, it is OK to make everything look flat, if that's what you want. Most important thing is to be consistent.

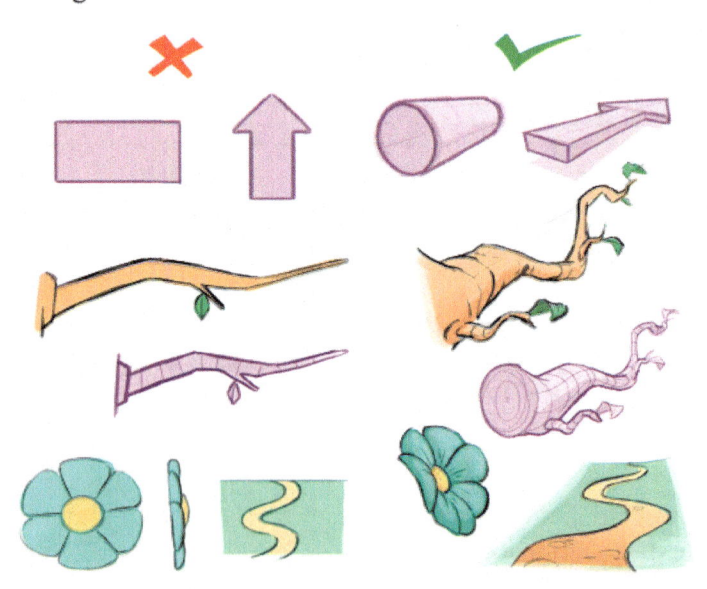

Drawing streets

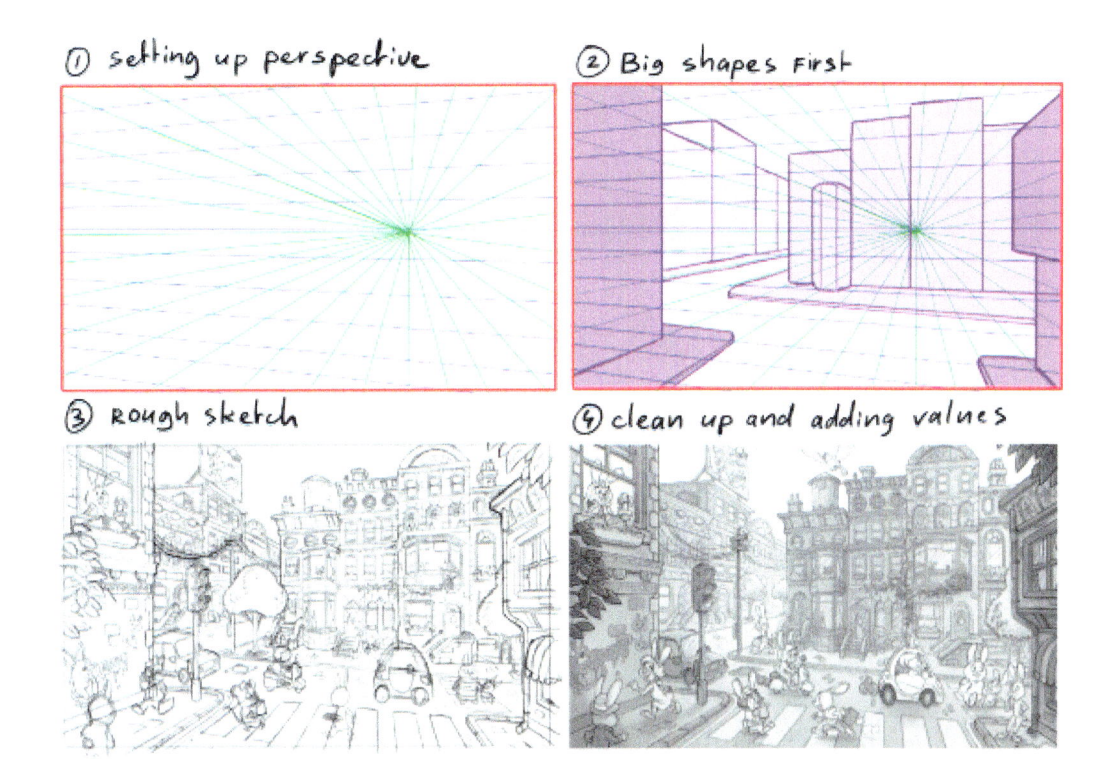

① setting up perspective ② Big shapes first

③ rough sketch ④ clean up and adding values

Drawing buildings and streets is a great way to start using perspective. Buildings have a lot of straight angles, like blocks. Conveniently, blocks are the easiest things to draw in perspective.

① Set the perspective

② big shapes first. Leave space for garden & vegetation

③ First sketch Rough on the big shapes

When I draw a street or a part of a city, I start drawing blocks like these. First the big shapes and after that I add smaller shapes.

Next step is adding the smaller shapes and details on the buildings.

45

Drawing a forest

Drawing a forest is different from drawing a city because you are drawing all these organic shapes. Still, it's good to think of those shapes in 3D and try to get a lot of depth in these drawings. That's why I draw these grids on top of it.

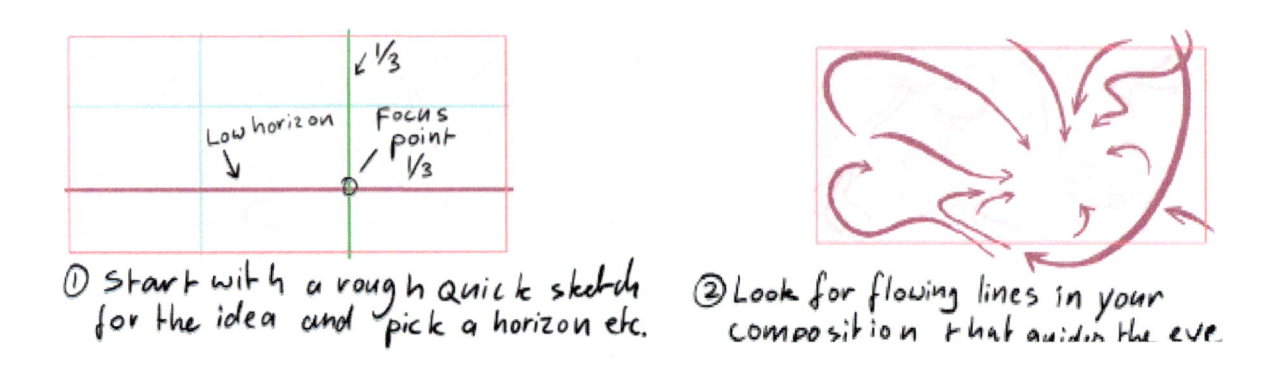

① Start with a rough quick sketch for the idea and pick a horizon etc.

② Look for flowing lines in your composition that guides the eye.

Here, I'm showing the step by step process of drawing a forest scene. I started with the composition, I used the rule of thirds (this is the composition rule I use most). After that, I look for the rhythm in the drawing by drawing on top of these lines.

③ Start sketching and follow the arrows

④ add values think in layers of depth fore, middle & background

⑤ adding core shadow to give everything more depth

⑥ add color. The foreground has the most saturation the back the least

After I put down the rhythm, I start sketching on top of the arrows, keeping it rough and loose. Once I got that, I work on the lines and start adding values. Most of the time, the values in the foreground are the darkest and the farther away they are, the lighter they get. This is because of atmospheric perspective. When that is done, I add the core shadows. Last step is to add colors, you can add the colors also in step 4. Depends on how you like to work.

Drawing mountains

You can draw mountains in many different ways. When you are drawing a scene, try to come up with different compositions and choose the one you like most.

Before you start on your final drawing, you can draw thumbnails. Thumbnails are quick little drawings that are quick to make and will save you time before you start working on the final drawing.

① create grid

② draw the room. Draw the ch as size ref

③ draw furniture

47

Drawing interiors

When drawing interiors, you draw the walls and the furniture. So, mostly square-shaped objects. I often start with a rough thumbnail to get an idea of what I want to draw. Once I have that, I make a grid that fits that thumbnail. After that, I can start drawing all the objects in the drawing.

④ smaller objects

⑦ draw in character to add life

⑤ draw over shapes

⑧ add colors

⑥ add values

⑨ Final touch

For this drawing I didn't use a frame or aspect ratio. I drew a box and put the room inside of it. This can be useful for production. For example, when they want to create a 3D environment. This way you can see most of the walls and get a good overview of the room. Also, take notice of how I first drew all the furniture as big shapes first

① setting up perspective

② Big shapes first   ③ Final line art

① draw the room first   ② Drawing tables as cubes

③ Final sketch

More examples of drawing interiors and how I draw the walls. First, I draw the longest wall (wall 1 in the picture) and then add the smaller walls to it.

① start with the perspective and create the big walls first

② build the smaller shapes

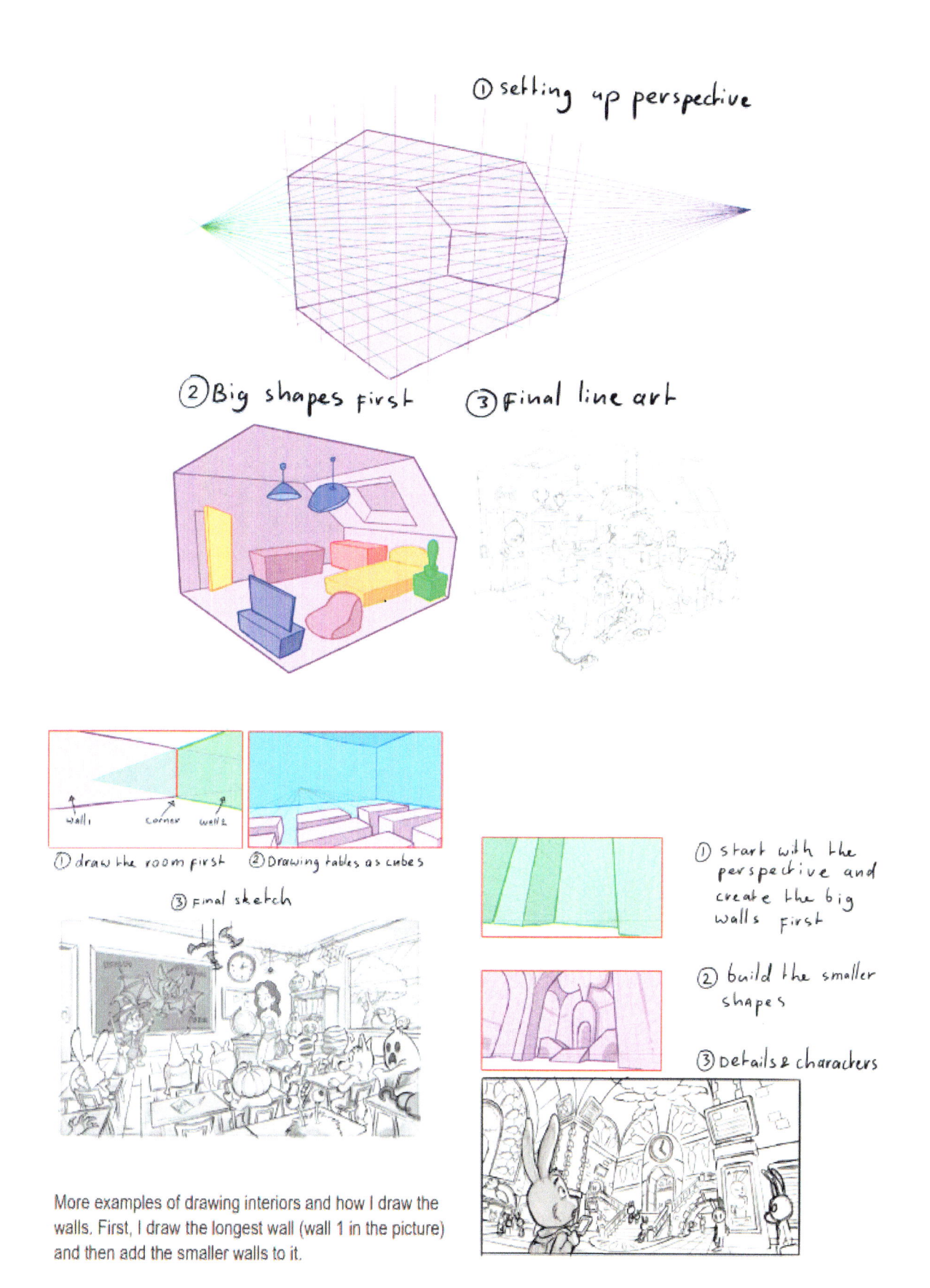

③ Details & characters

DRAWING PROPS

Introduction to props

A prop is an object in an environment. A prop can be a car, lamp, clock, chair, carpet, plant, etc. An interior has a lot of props. Try to design the props using fun and dynamic proportions, look out they don't look stiff and dull.

Often, when I design an environment, I also design some of the key props separately. Because when you make them separately first you can give more thought to the design of the objects.

In the case of a 3D project, all these props need to be modelled as well. So sometimes, drawings from each prop are needed as well .

Drawing a car

1. start with a rough sketch (15 min)

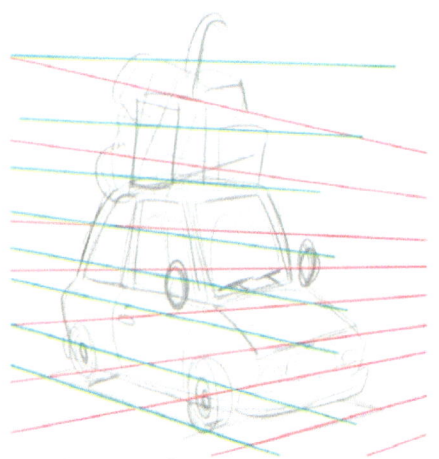

2. add on top of the rough sketch a two point perspective (5 min)

A car is also a prop. In this illustration I show a step by step process of drawing a car. I start with a rough drawing and when I like that, I start adding perspective on top of it and work on the final sketch.

3. draw the final linework on top of the perspective lines (20 min)

4. ink the lines and add color on it (20 min)
total time 60 minutes

Srawing a spaceship .

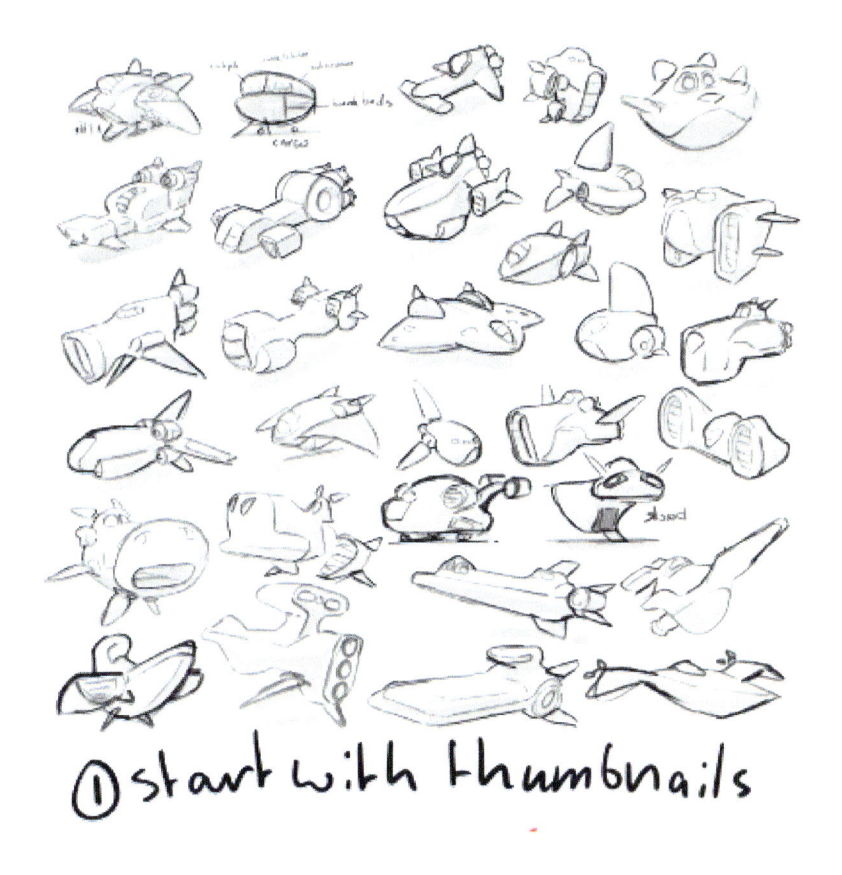

In the first image you can see my process of doodling or making thumbnails. Basically, these are quick doodles that aren't too complicated, so I can make a lot of them. I try to push the designs as far and crazy as I can. If one of these little drawings breaks because I've gone too far, it doesn't really matter because it didn't took me too much time.

Once I found the perfect thumbnail, I start adding perspective etc.

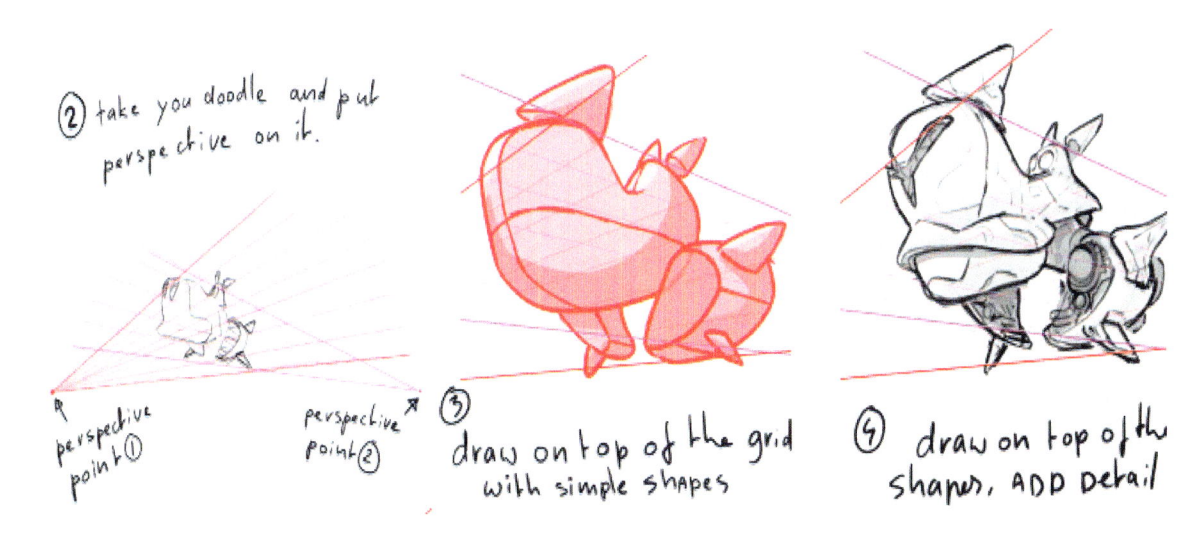

Drawing a boat

Another example of some thumbnails. I made even more, but I selected these ones to add to my portfolio. When you are working for a client, you don't have to send all your thumbnails. Just send the ones you like the most and consider adding contrasting examples.

I added a character to the drawing to give it more life and make it more fun. I also wanted to show different angles as well as the interior of the boat. This gives an idea of what the boat looks like and how the puffin lives on the boat

Drawing clouds

Drawing clouds can be harder than it looks. Because they are so simple, it's really important to get the principles right. In the example I show that I start with a small shape, a medium shape and a big shape. I do that to keep the shape interesting and appealing. For that reason, I also apply straight vs curved lines at the top and bottom of the cloud. It's all about contrast.

LEARN MORE

Fill a page with completely different clouds an go crazy with all the shapes and proportions. See how far you can push it.

Clouds in perspective :
You can draw clouds as cubes first if you want to draw them in perspective. It helps you getting the overall perspective right .

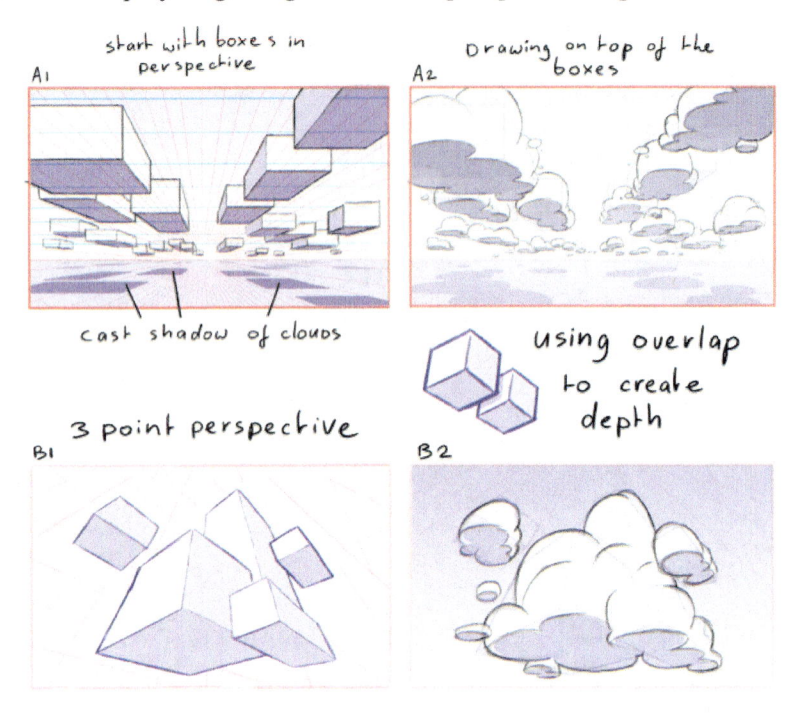

A1 start with boxes in perspective
A2 Drawing on top of the boxes
cast shadow of clouds

B1 3 point perspective
B2 using overlap to create depth

Composition and clouds :
Clouds are great to make an interesting composition in your drawing. They are great for this because you can lead the eye to the subject that is important for the composition.

use clouds for flow

use clouds to frame

Diagonal direction

Different ways to frame

clouds from above

clouds around the mountain

56

Drawing trees :
Trees come in all sizes and shapes. Look at trees and try to break them up in shapes. In my cartoony style I often look at real trees and use these as a reference, when I start drawing I push them as much as I want to make an interesting design.

Try to keep it simple. Work from big shapes to small shapes. Take one step at a time. Like starting with the trunk and adding a big shape for the leaves. In that big shape you can add all the branches.

To make a tree more interesting, you can add a twist to the trunk or branches, to make it more dynamic.

Learn more!

It's really fun to go crazy with tree shapes. I challenge you to fill a page with different trees. Try to make them as different as possibe, think in contrast.

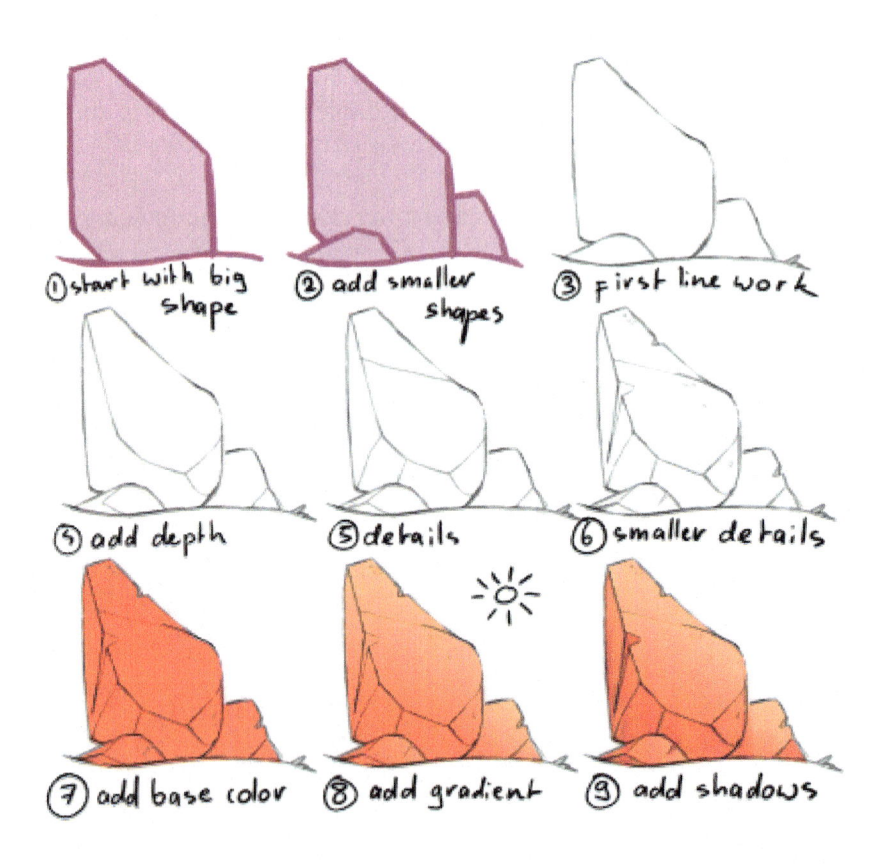

Drawing rocks

What I like about drawing rocks is that they can be both organic and a bit geometric shaped at the same time. The variations are endless! Start with drawing big shapes first. A lot of times I'm working with three shapes. Earlier I mentiond the power of three. So, often I play around with a big shape, medium shape and a small shape.

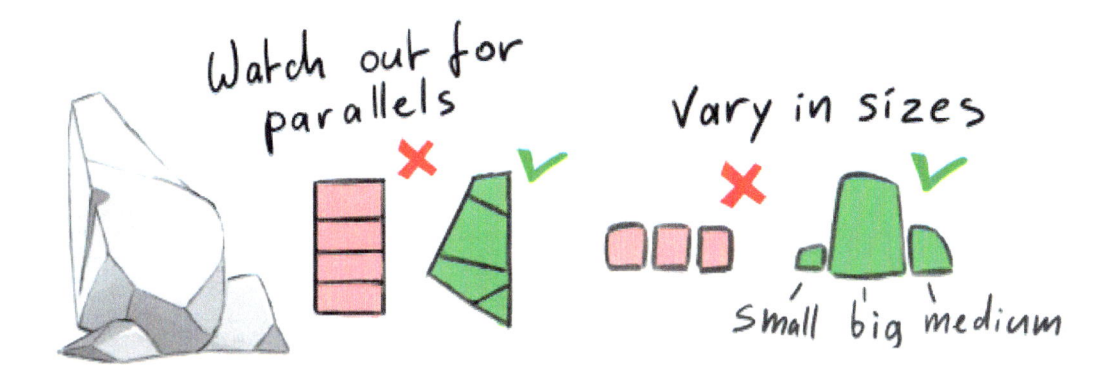

Here, you can see how the power of three works. Also try to avoid parallel lines because that doesn't look natural.

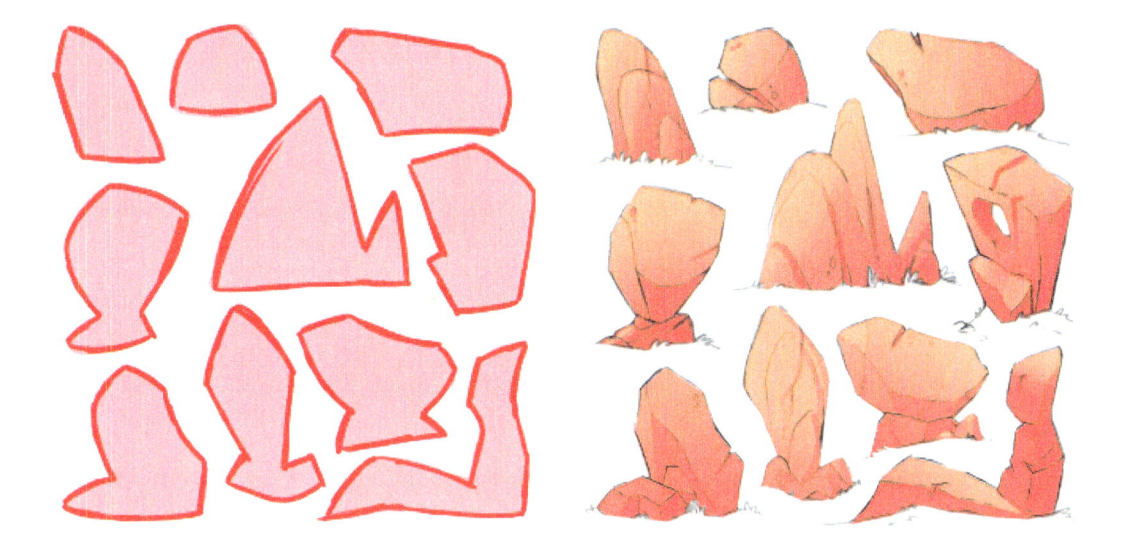

Learn more!

Try to draw as many different rocks on one page as you can. Always push yourself to go for the biggest diversity. Think in big shapes first and later divide them in three smaller shapes.

Creating Effects

Do's & don'ts

  This image demonstrates 'wrong' and 'right'. To be honest, there is no wrong and right so you shouldn't take this literally. Sometimes, some productions use the "wrong" version deliberately. Shows like Family Guy are using a lot of parallels and straight lines. But they do that for a purpose. So, decide what your goal is. I want to make lively, dynamic, cartoony worlds, that's why I like try to add contrast.

Effect types : Smoke and fire are moving on air. So, think about how they move
through the air. Hot air goes up and pushes cold air downwards, so wind is created. You also see this effect in smoke and fire

60

Drawing explosions

Explosions are a force that pushes outwards. So, think of your shape as though every part of it is moving outwards. That is how I start. I start with these big shapes and think about the force creating the shape. Refer to the example on how I do that. In image (2) you see that I divided these bigger shapes into smaller circles that are pushed together and are moving outwards.

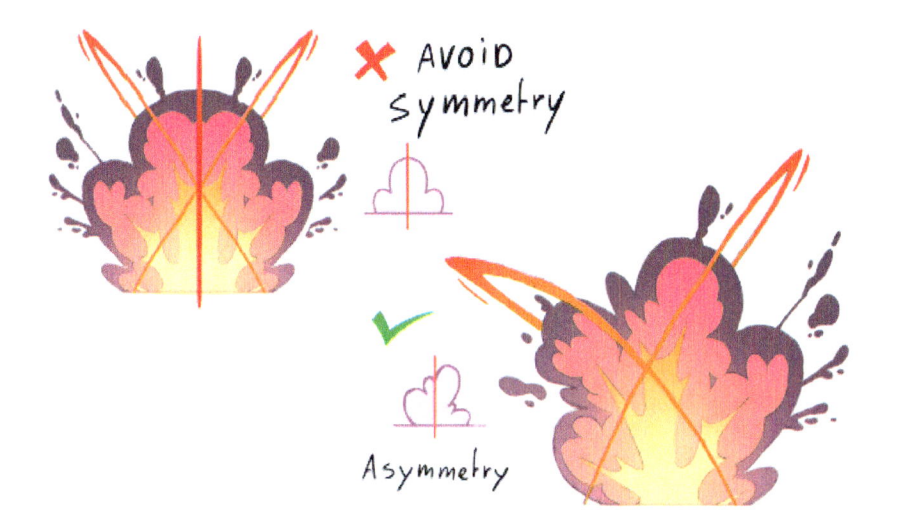

Avoid symmetry

When you are making an explosion, it is tempting to make it symmetrical. For some reason, people like symmetry but symmetry is not something to be found in nature that often. So, pay attention to this when drawing an explosion, try to avoid an artificial shape.

Drawing thunder

With drawing thunder it's really important to make it irregular. Try to make it as random as possible and use short, middle and long lines. Try to fil a page full with different thunder and look for the one that is the most natural looking. Thunder is chaos and every thunder strike is completely different

① start with big line

ADD ② secondary lines

③ ADD smaller lines

Drawing water

Splashing water is also driven by a force, just like an explosion. Only is it in this case aimed at a direction. So you can see on the arrows that it is pushed towards a certain direction. I also drew it like it is hitting an object. You see the water/force bouncing of it.

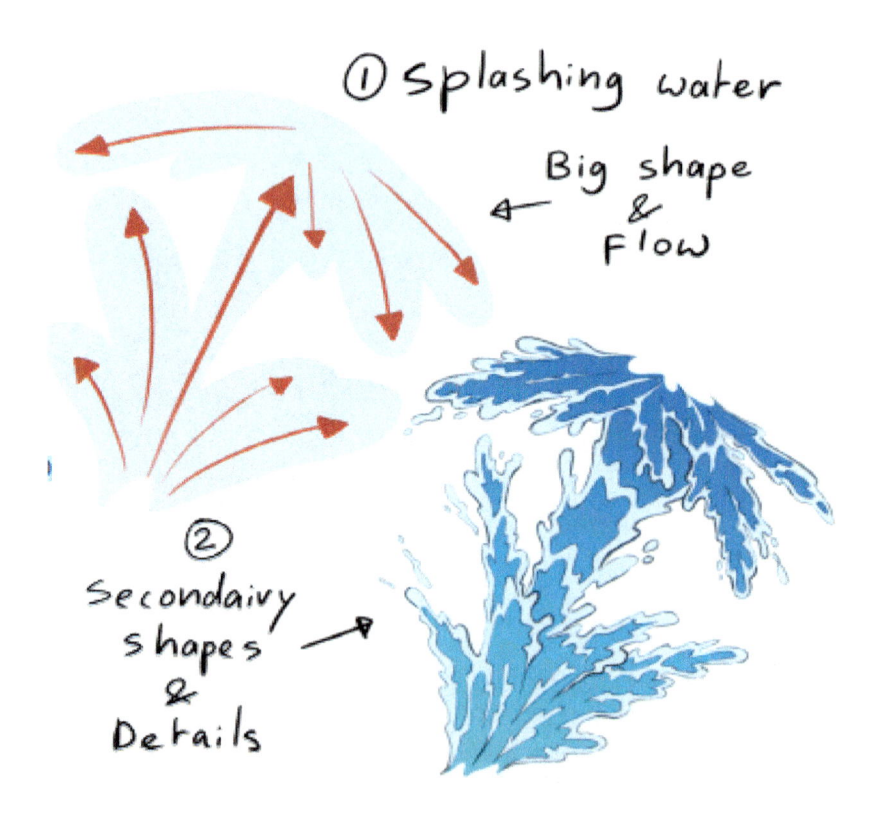

① Splashing water

Big shape & Flow

② Secondairy shapes & Details

Drawing smoke

Here you can see smoke rising up. Notice that the smoke rotates when it moves upwards. That is because of the phenomenon of hot air pushing cold air downwards, which I talked about in regards to the explosion. This rotating movement also makes it dynamic.

Avoid symmetry

Avoid symmetry in smoke by playing around with shapes. Even a simple swinging tail of smoke can be asymmetrical. Try to push both ends to be as contrasting as possible. It depends on the style you want how far you should push that.

Drawing Backgrounds

In this example I'm showing the basic steps. First, set your composition, add line work, add values and lastly add colors. Following these steps will help you to focus on each area separately. That's why I like to do the values before I add colors, so I can focus on getting the values right first.

Drawing a background from a – z

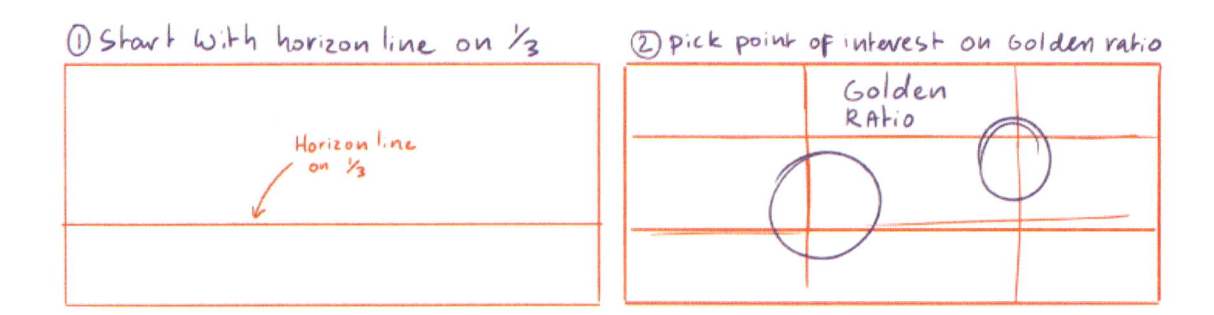

① Start with horizon line on ⅓

Horizon line on ⅓

② Pick point of interest on Golden ratio

Golden Ratio

I always start with the canvas and add the horizon line. Most of the time, I put the horizon line on 1/3 or 2/3 of the drawing because that will result in the most appealing composition. Once I've done that, I decide where to put the focus points on the crossings of the 1/3 grid.

③ ADD perspective, big shapes first

perspective

And once that is done, I start deciding on the perspective and add all the big shapes first. At this stage, I really focus on creating 3D shapes with volume and space. In this example I pushed them inwards to convey a feeling of depth and dimension. Once those big shapes are put into perspective, I start drawing roughly on top of it.

④ ADD perspective to smaller shapes

Once I'm satisfied with the rough sketch, I start cleaning up the drawing and start inking. Once that is done, I add colors to it. This step depends a bit on my decision to either render the image or to use cell shading on it.

1. I start with a rough sketch
2. clean the sketch up
3. start inking with a hard brush
4. start adding colors in layers
5. add shadow & details
   - multiply layer
   - color on layer
   - think of color scheme

Here is an example of the steps from sketch to finish. These are the steps I usually take, but everyone has his or hers own type of workflow.

Srawing a harbor

These are my first thumbnails that turn into a sketch. I start really simple almost abstract and add more details along the way. At this stage, I eyeball the perspective .

① I start with simple thumbnails like this

② put the horizon line on ⅓

③ start adding shapes

③ DRAW over the sketh loosely

Once I've put down the first sketch I put the perspective on top of it. I change some things to optimize the perspective and I fix any mistakes I made while eyeballing the perspective. Be careful at this stage, if you focus too much on getting the perspective right, it can start looking stiff .

④ start adding perspective

⑤ sketch details

Here you can see what the sketch looks like in perspective. I tried to add perspective that is right and solid, but I also wanted to keep the energy of the sketch.

Once I'm happy with the sketch, I start inking. Inking can be hard because it can totally ruin a good sketch, but it can also save a bad sketch. It is important to take your time for this stage.

⑥ Final linework

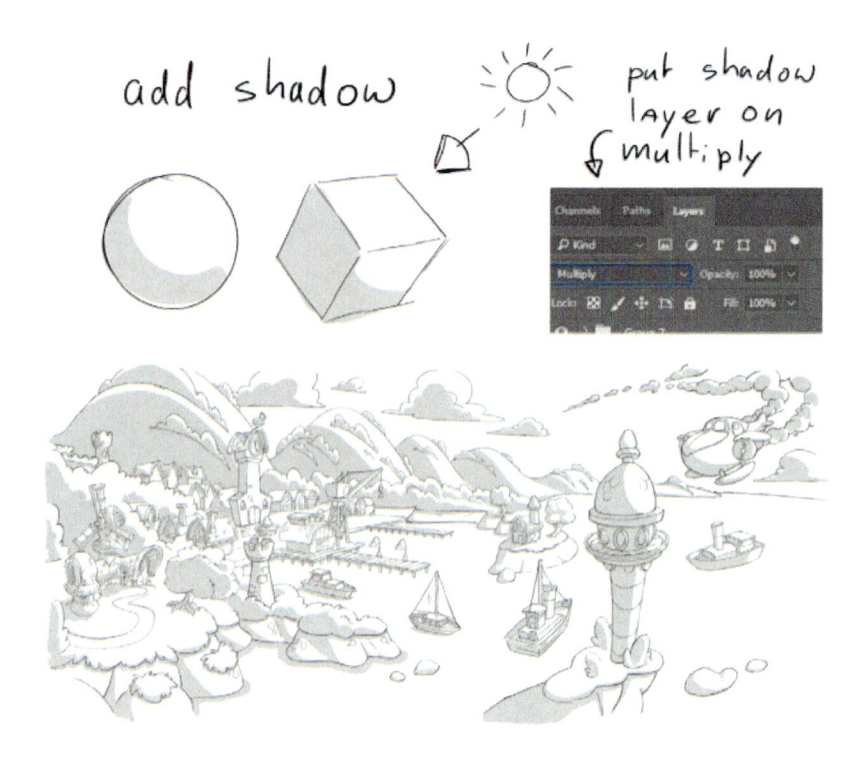

Once I finish inking, I start adding shadows. In this case, I choose cell shaded shading. This means that I add a hard shadow layer on top of the colors. In Photoshop, I set this layer to multiply mode .

Once I've added shadows, I start adding colors. I'm using a basic color scheme. Once I'm satisfied, I put the shadow layer on top of it. And that combination makes this finished drawing.

You can choose to soften the shadow and add lighting. It all depends on what kind of style you want to get.

1. starting with rough shapes

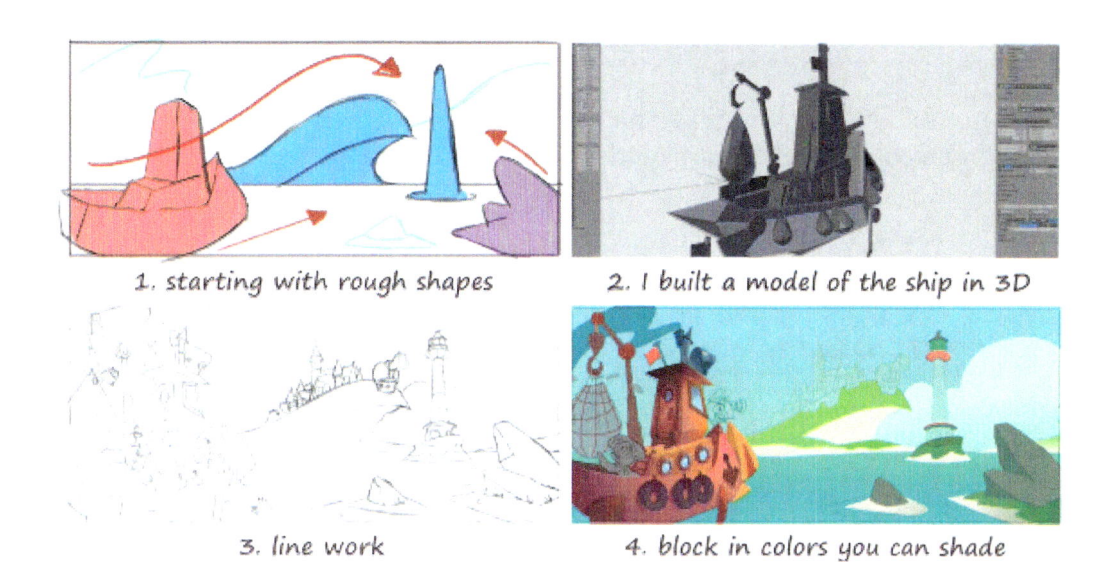

2. I built a model of the ship in 3D

3. line work

4. block in colors you can shade

Using 3D

Making a rough model of some of your elements in 3D can be quite help full when you are setting up a scene. In this example, I only made the boat in 3D and put it in the right perspective. Then, I screenshot it and placed it inside the 2D environment.

When I create a new scene with the same boat, I simply rotate the boat in the 3D software, screenshot it again an place it in the new environment.

5. adding shading, adding details, adding texture and color tweaks

Creating a portfolio piece

This is an example of how I create a portfolio piece. If you want to apply for a job at an animation studio as an environment artist or set designer, I would advise you to create something like this.

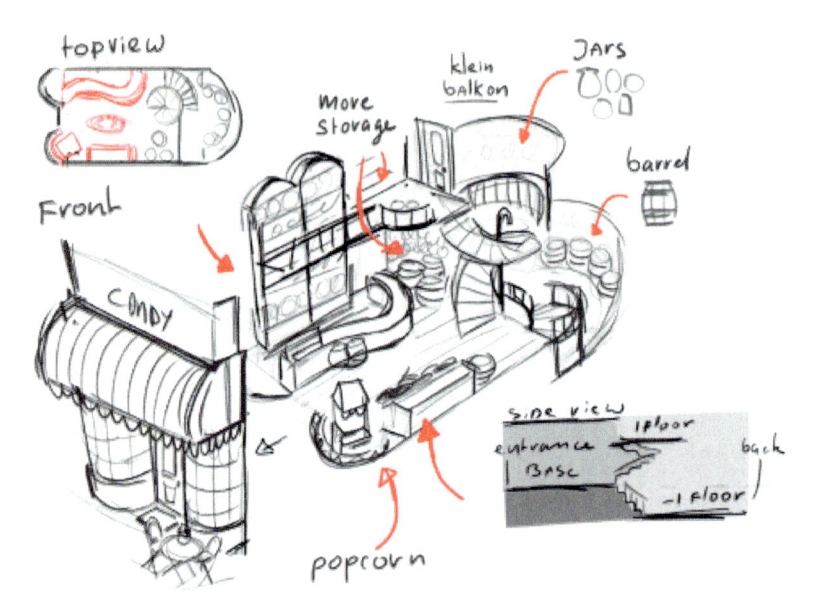

I always start with a floor plan or an isometric drawing. While sketching roughly, I start thinking of the design of the interior. I try to think of as much as I can think of. I do that to avoid having to think of it in a later stage. So, this is your planning stage. Try to be rough and don't worry about clean lines.

Once I made a floor plan, I like I start making a cleaned up isometric view. This will give me a good idea of how it's going to be. An isometric view also helps later on as a map of where to put everything in different shots.

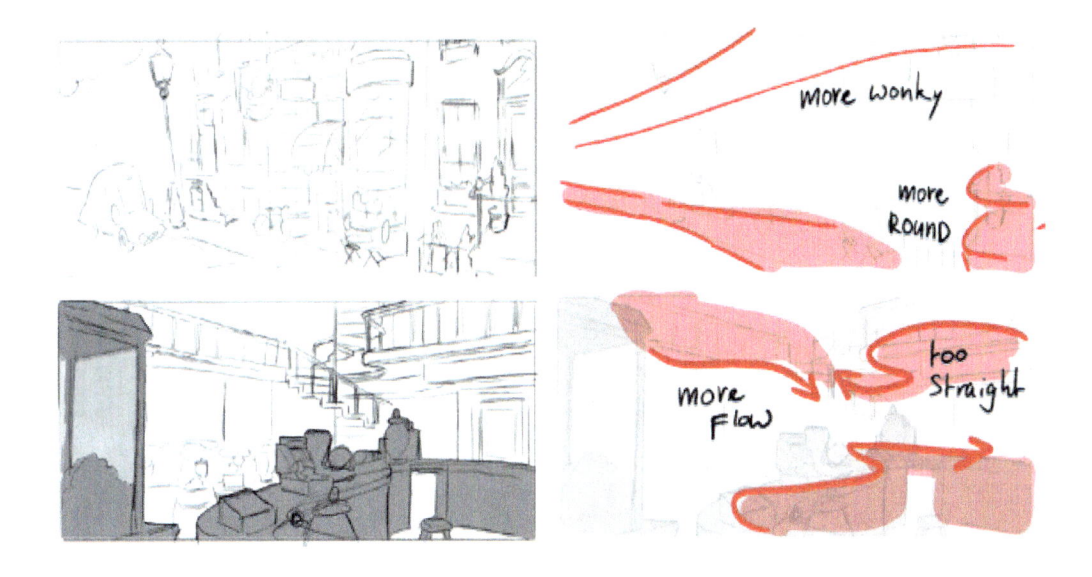

After I made the floor plan, I start sketching thumbnails for the final drawings. Try to be rough and quick. It's really putting ideas on paper. At this stage, I start to think about composition, rhythm and storytelling. Sometimes I go back to the isometric stage and change some things. It's still OK to change stuff at this stage because everything is still relatively rough.

At some animation studios they expect that the environment artist also makes 3D mock-ups. The 3D is used at the planning stage and for the animation. Once they approve it, a specialized 3D artist will pick it up and model it for real. So, if you want to work for animation studios it can't hurt to learn at least some basics of 3D. When you have made a model like this you can also figure out more easily what shots you should use.

Here you see the final line draw over on the 3D models. The great thing of using 3D is that the software creates the perspective for you. When drawing over it, you'll have perfect perspective. Be aware of stiffness when you use this technique. You can avoid this by adding some wonky stuff. Like with the candy store everything is handmade and therefore not perfectly straight and uneven.

I also made these drawings in really high resolution and with clear lines so people can zoom in on a particular object. This is very convenient for 3D modelers if they want to model an object.

I export the renders from the 3D software with lighting, so I won't have to think about that when adding light and shadows. Lastly, underneath the line layer, I paint with brushes and gradient tools .

LEARN MORE .

Create your own portfolio piece now! Start with a basic idea, I simply choose a candy store because they're cheerful, have a lot of jars and objects to fill a room. The great thing about the jars is that you can easily duplicate them! Also attach the sketches to your portfolio project. This shows that you can come up with multiple ideas.

Printed in Great Britain
by Amazon